Beauty as Action

Beauty as Action

How Practicing True Beauty Can Change Our World

Lisa Z. Lindahl

“Messenger” by Mary Oliver reprinted with permission.

ISBN: 0998746703
ISBN 13: 9780998746708

Contents

Messenger

My work is loving the world.
Here the sunflowers, there the hummingbird–
equal seekers of sweetness.
Here the quickening yeast; there the blue plums.
Here the clam deep in the speckled sand.
Are my boots old? Is my coat torn?
Am I no longer young, and still not half-perfect? Let me
keep my mind on what matters,
which is my work,

which is mostly standing still and learning to be
astonished.
The phoebe, the delphinium.
The sheep in the pasture, and the pasture.
Which is mostly rejoicing, since all the ingredients are here,

which is gratitude, to be given a mind and a heart
and these body-clothes,
a mouth with which to give shouts of joy
to the moth and the wren, to the sleepy dug-up clam,
telling them all, over and over, how it is
that we live forever.

–Mary Oliver

Introduction

THE NATURE OF True Beauty (making the distinction from the cosmetics counter) and its significance in our everyday lives is what this book is about. Bringing such beauty into our daily routines, recognizing the True Beauty already existing in our lives, and experiencing its powerful effects—this is at the heart of *Beauty As Action: How Practicing True Beauty Can Change Our World.*

It was winter, I recall, and my business partner and I were driving north up a gray Interstate 89 from Montpelier, Vermont's capital. We were returning from yet another all-important meeting. She was driving my beat-up, old Volkswagen Beetle—and jabbering, jabbering, going over and over and *over* the meeting. I felt the car's small interior thick with intense energy, strained with expectations, of each other, of our fledgling business, of ourselves. The forty-five-minute drive back to our office in Burlington was getting more uncomfortable for me with every mile.

To our left, the early-setting sun unexpectedly erupted between the snow-laden clouds and the distant Adirondack Mountains, momentarily dazzling our roadside surroundings with startling pinks and golds. Sunrays caught dark treetops, transforming them into glowing fingers of color and light, then ran across the land toward the highway and our gas-powered capsule of human intensity.

"Beauty break! Beauty break!" I cried out without thinking, interrupting the tirade beside me, seeking, I knew, a brief reprieve from her concentrated single-mindedness. "Look! Look at that light on the hills! Look at our sunset!" She glanced over, saw, and smiled. Her shoulders relaxed.

Thus has it ever been for me, and I believe for others who stop to notice: beauty, *True* Beauty, lifts us up. Releases us. And that is just the beginning of True Beauty's happy effects.

When, years later, I sold that business, I took some time out to think about what really—I mean *really*—matters. In that liminal space between what had been and what was yet to come, there was that opportunity to ask myself the biggie: the *existential question,* all capital letters in my head.

What came up for me was beauty.

I don't mean that shallow bit that is all about appearances and cosmetics—but those things of eternal beauty, authentic True Beauty. I remember clearly the moment this thought first struck me.

I was in my studio office, standing at the window that overlooked Lake Champlain. It was the end-of-winter-not-quite-spring time of year in Vermont known as mud season—a difficult and trying time for souls yearning for sunshine's warmth and small-growing green things. Looking out the window, I noticed that the gray day was lifting and just enough midday light was filtering through to create sparkle on the lake water as it busily chopped about. A blue jay's call suddenly pierced my reverie, and I was enveloped by a sense of timeless and complete beauty.

Then the thought broke through: Beauty! Beauty is what really matters!

Huh?

In that first moment, I did not understand. The thought, what I had sensed, what did it really mean? I felt its importance, its essentialness. It was as if I saw an inviting vista in front of me, a portal into a landscape that I could not quite wholly comprehend. I recognized an opportunity; a beautiful, mysterious place beckoned me forward to investigate.

Honestly, it also seemed a farfetched notion. But I could not let it go. I realized how much natural beauty in my surroundings had been an influence in my life, my decisions.

Over time, I began noticing how this "beauty" cropped up in ways other than visual, other than in the natural world. And I found myself embarking upon an exploration of this vision, of what I came to call True Beauty and the Way of Beauty.

It took some years, but I came to understand more fully my window-side experience. As I did so, I perceived the great healing power of this eternal dynamic, this True Beauty, and that it is extremely important to reclaim True Beauty now. Now! We must do this for our own health, both physically and spiritually, for the health of our planet and to help create and maintain balance in our global communities. Sound like a big order? True Beauty is the key.

And so I invite you to join me on your own journey of discovery. To consider "beauty" and *release* how you may have previously perceived it. Then enter this eternal landscape and consider what it has to offer, and next—most importantly—to encounter and experiment with True Beauty, to actually try practicing True Beauty! To see how "beauty" can be a verb and is, truly, *action.*

By practicing beauty, we become partners in creating harmony in our universe.

This is how the book is, in fact, structured. We start out looking at the broad vista of beauty, reviewing the landscape, so to speak. Then, stepping on the path—the "Way of Beauty"—where stories are told to illustrate or embellish upon a particular beauty practice and take us forward on each step of the journey. As Muriel Rukeyser said, "The universe is made of stories, not atoms."

Though all the practices build upon one another, they also stand alone. There is no one linear way to practice True Beauty. In one practice, I might refer to a previous practice simply because they relate to and inform one another. Yet we could open up the book to any practice and just start doing it!

Then, at the end of the journey of discovery and practicing, we pause and reflect to think about the implications of the journey and to see how certain things might change or be impacted by True Beauty. We'll see how we need not feel overwhelmed by all the personal and sociopolitical issues assaulting us now—that we are not helpless individuals in the face of these problems.

Practicing beauty makes us partners in creating harmony in our universe. *Partners.* This is where the "beauty as action" journey takes us.

A brief aside—while doing the research that evolved into this book, some of the material I encountered was deeply scientific, philosophical, and sometimes academic and existential. Both the sciences and history support the relevance and importance of True Beauty, as opposed to mere glamour, in our lives today. When I first started writing about beauty in relation to some of these historical or theoretical areas, I sometimes felt like I was back teaching in a classroom, and I worried things were sounding a bit, uh, *dry*. Yet I could not write a book about the nature and importance of True Beauty without the inclusion of at least a few of these supporting and validating threads. I hope these enrich and deepen the subject matter for you and don't send you running for a glass of water!

> *The timelessness of beauty saves us from worshipping at the shrine of progress or kneeling at the altar to pray that tomorrow we will make more money than today…beauty has nothing to do with progress. Who will be so rash as to proclaim that our present buildings are more beautiful than the Parthenon…our present churches more beautiful than Chartres…our modern music better than Mozart and Bach? Beauty is beyond the confines of progress…The one thing we can be sure about is the timelessness of beauty…*
>
> ROLLO MAY, MY QUEST FOR BEAUTY

Part One

The Landscape of True Beauty

True Beauty: The Bridge between the Many and the One

WE HAVE HAD Western philosophies and Eastern philosophies, Aboriginal wisdom, and women's wisdom. We have turned common wisdom into "folklore," and sometimes I think common sense has become a lost art.

In our information age, much has become available all at once to label, compare, and contrast. All that was OK; one can suppose it a step in the evolution. Yet for some time now it's been observed that although we have much access to information, we are losing the wisdom with which to process it. In fact during his pre-computer lifetime, poet and Nobel Laureate T.S. Eliot (1888-1965) asked the question: "Where is the wisdom we have lost in knowledge? Where is the knowledge we have lost in information?"

Now it is time to evolve into the next generation of awareness, a generation that pursues not just information, but wisdom, and on that path acknowledges unity consciousness while fully celebrating the fabulous and intriguing individuation of life. For it is *life,* that magical force of life, that unifies us all.

There has occurred a breach, a separation and polarization between our consciousness and what I refer to as "The Isness," what the ancient Vedic tradition calls "Brahman," a single whole. It is called many things in many belief systems. To me, it is that which is *true, central, core, and real,* no matter what the language or consciousness level.

Recognizing, reclaiming, and practicing True Beauty will kick-start and nourish the emergent evolution.

The Isness transcends all languages, all dogmas, and cultural barriers. Smiles and laughter are universal, as is the experience of the truly beautiful—however it may appear or be perceived. Yet a forgetfulness makes us disown this knowingness.

Why do we stray? Why do we forget? These are rhetorical questions, really. What is happening now in certain circles on the planet is a recognition that the current paradigm, or operating principles, *must shift.* Humankind must change our ways. It is my hypothesis that by simply healing this one fundamental pathology—the abandonment and trivialization of beauty—much else would fall into place; much else will *heal.*

A Manifesto for True Beauty

All contemporary crises can be reduced to a crisis about the nature of beauty.
—John O'Donohue

Polarizing dualities can't exist, and luscious diversity may unashamedly bloom in a universe where True Beauty is a primary paradigm and one of humankind's guiding references.

This is true for me.

I want to make it true for the majority of humankind. Why? Read on.

The ancient Greeks revered beauty. "The teleology of the Universe is directed to the production of Beauty," declared the father of process philosophy, Alfred North Whitehead. "Beauty prompts action," said author James Hillman. "Beauty must replicate itself," stated Harvard's professor of aesthetics, Elaine Scarry.

"So what?" any skeptic may ask. "How is *beauty* relevant in a world burdened with wars, starvation, and an increasing gap between the uberwealthy and the rest of us—not to mention the truly poor?" For many, beauty is trivial and nonessential, and its serious pursuit is a shallow endeavor.

I say otherwise. Yes, in our modern times, beauty has become caricatured, trivialized, and marginalized to an extreme and ridiculous level. It has been relegated to the shallows of the naïve and romantic, while the mass media elevates and enshrines mere glamour and the bad news of violence, greed, crime, and coarseness.

To skeptics I say this: You are confusing True Beauty with glamour. And no wonder, as our society is doing so as well.

And glamour? Glamour is a trick, an illusion. It is defined as such in our dictionaries. Glamour is a bright flash and—poof!—gone. Glamour has no substance. As one beauty commentator, poet John O'Donohue, put it, "It has become the habit of our times to mistake glamour for beauty."

Throughout our recent cultural past, the lowest common denominator has become the highest thing to aspire to. These days, elegance and graciousness are often derided and dismissed while mediocrity and baseness are somehow socially desirable.

So how am I defining beauty, or what I refer to as *True Beauty*?

It is not about appearances, or *merely* about appearance; it is that which is *eternal*, though its expression may be ephemeral. It is that which resonates in *harmony* with another, though it exists independently.

For instance, an eternal expression of and response to True Beauty is laughter. A tree, a night sky, the scent of honeysuckle—the natural world is truly, eternally beautiful. How we see it, how we depict it, however, is catching a moment in time, perceived by one individual lens.

While laughter is the same in every language and culture, human responses and expressions of True Beauty vary greatly, and others may well not find all such expressions "beautiful," something this book explores.

Out beyond ideas of wrong-doing
& right-doing
There is a field
I'll meet you there.
When the soul lies down in that grass
The world is too full to talk about.

–Jalal ad-Din Rumi

Beauty *grabs* us. Upon first noticing beauty, we might tend to observe it as "other"—me/it, subject/object. Then we are pulled in, aren't we? There is a vibration we resonate with, and in fact, we do start vibrating with the beauty, entrain with it. In this way, we become a part of the beauty, of the harmony being created, a part of a harmonic convergence, if you will.

And we are often changed as a result. Sometimes the experience is so brief it goes almost unnoticed. A quick scent floats in and out. A sudden shaft of light comes into our environment. And perhaps we are unconsciously healed in ways and places we did not know were injured or needed to be "polished up." Other times, an experience of True Beauty makes us very aware of its power to shift our being.

Author Rollo May (*The Courage to Create* and *Love and Will*) had his "aha!" experience of the healing power of True Beauty when out walking one day. Coming around a slight hill, he chanced upon an unexpected field of wild poppies standing vividly scarlet against the bright-blue sky. The sight literally *jolted* him out of a deep depression he had been battling for some time.

Even such a chance encounter with True Beauty can change the direction of our lives and our world. True Beauty is powerful.

The current lack of understanding about the importance of authentic beauty in humankind's cultures, its suppression and repression over the past two centuries especially, has led to the societal pathologies that are festering and sickening us. There is a direct correlation between True Beauty's decline and the degradation of our civilization.

I want to say and say it loudly: Beauty is essential; it is what *really* matters. Beauty is the eternal divine, the source, and inspiration, the reason for *all.*

So here I am in deep waters: *the sea of larger implications.* To wit—beauty is the reason for the universe to be. "What?!" you might think. But don't be so quick to dismiss the notion. Go with me down this road for a bit, and let's see what we come up with. Sometimes the most simple and obvious is, in fact, the answer to the most complex-seeming equation. "The very simple and the highly complex are reflections of each other… Insights about the paradox of simplicity and complexity occur repeatedly in art and ancient wisdom." (Briggs and Peat, *Seven Life Lessons of Chaos: Spiritual Wisdom from the Science of Change.*)

They are the great existential questions: Why are we here? Why/how did the universe come into being, the big bang theory notwithstanding? Why does the universe continue to expand? And what is the nature of the intelligence behind all this design, behind the order that reveals itself underlying the chaos?

Many of us humans are happy to encapsulate such questions and their attendant concepts within the word "God"—and then spend lifetimes and much creative energy devising all the stuff to both describe and limit that God.

Others believe in random science and probabilities, with no organizing intelligence at the helm. Many others prefer not to think about it at all. They are content being told what to think when occasion necessitates. Others don't even know there's something to think about or not think about. Sometimes I think they are really the blessed ones: "Ignorance is bliss!"

In considering our global socioeconomic stresses, the state of our planet and its immediate atmosphere, as well as the theories of probabilities and potentialities—I know that the need to stop ignoring and repressing beauty has gone beyond its peak. The tipping point has come and gone. We must reinstate the importance of beauty in all things, intentions, and actions. We must do so *now.*

And while we will look at some definitions of True Beauty and its parameters, it is vital to note at the outset that authentic beauty, True Beauty, goes far beyond what only our senses may measure or what treasures money will buy, far beyond appearances of things, especially the human face and form.

Beauty as Action and its Way of Beauty aspire to transcend notions of standard "taste" as well as what each of us finds beautiful. Rather it seeks to elevate, honor, and call attention to the importance of that moment of engagement—that moment of "Wow…*so beautiful*!"—an experience we have all had.

Noticing and embracing the experiences of beauty in our lives is a step toward our own strengthening and, I propose, healing much of the existing cultural pathology that has arisen during the past century, the era of True Beauty's demise.

Now is the time to reclaim True Beauty. *Now.* It is extremely important.

Think about this statement. I believe we will all feel far less helpless about the state of our planet and its cultures once we see and understand this importance of True Beauty: how easy it is to have it in our everyday lives, its profound implications for building a harmonic civilization and perhaps most importantly,how each of us individually make a difference -- by simply practicing True Beauty.

True Beauty goes far beyond what only our senses may measure, what treasures money will buy, far beyond mere appearance.

Beauty is the practice that can heal humankind's present situation and return our world and our role within it to a positive and regenerative one. Through a practice of True Beauty, we can evolve and expand our consciousness and be a productive, elegant, and facilitative element in the universe as it proceeds in continually rebirthing itself.

You cannot hope to build a better world
without improving the individuals.
To that end each of us must work
for his own improvement.
—Marie Curie

Defining True Beauty

The perfection of Beauty is defined as being the perfection of Harmony.
—Alfred North Whitehead

What is "beauty"? It is not a gorgeous day and a free meal with dessert, preferably chocolate. Let me restate that; it is not only that.

I will start by arguing that, in philosophical terms, beauty, True Beauty, is concrete. We've turned it into a plethora of abstractions and then focused upon them, losing sight of the concrete principle that birthed them. Beauty is far from merely pleasing appearances. While beauty can, of course, manifest in form and appearance, it also exists as function, feeling, spirit, and what I refer to as the *integral isness*. With this in mind, one will find definitions of beauty sprinkled throughout this text, in accordance with whatever facet of the topic we are exploring.

A seminal aspect of the sort of beauty we are exploring is harmony. Experiencing beauty in great part is about resonating with the harmonies occurring in our perceptions, whether of the physical senses or the energetic fields. Identifying and perceiving beauty is having an interactive experience of harmony. So, what is harmony?

Like the term *beauty* itself, *harmony*, too, is a word that has become overused, glossed over, and often only partially understood.

Simply, harmony is two or more parts that fit and/or flow together with grace. Being in sync with. In the groove and in the flow. At one with. Hence, beauty is about relationships (the "with factor") in dynamic harmony. "Dynamic" is the operative word here. Without this dynamic beauty, our ever-expanding universe could not resolve into itself.

Relationship, also, is key in True Beauty. One might ask, "Doesn't there have to be an 'other' to be in relationship with?" Well, one might answer: "Aren't we in relationship with ourselves? Do we converse with ourselves and self-reflect? Doesn't a living system have a feedback loop?"

Harmony by its very definition is finding concord among several entities, it is integral in constructive relationship. In the obvious example of music, those entities are differentiated as notes, acoustic waves resonating at differing vibratory frequencies, creating different individual sounds that when they come together will result in either cacophony or harmony.

When the term *harmony* is applied outside of music, we take it to mean anything or things that come together in a pleasing way.

Harmony is the expression of True Beauty. So I might say, "True Beauty is about the pursuit of harmony in all actions and interactions of our daily living." This sounds a bit friendlier than this: harmony is about integrating and correlating diverse pieces and parts to create congruent entities resulting in True Beauty.

Think of the oil whisked into vinegar to create the tangy taste of vinaigrette, or of yellow pigment infused with some blue to create a lovely green paint—these are harmonies. Conversely, cacophony will result from mixing that vinegar in with the yellow pigment...yuk! Got nothing there—to eat or paint with!

What does harmony feel like? Who has ever said, "I'm feeling a bit harmonic today?" Silly, huh? Yet I think we translate harmony into a sense of contentment, the grounds for happiness.

Being contented, in the time, place, and era I grew up in (I'm a boomer), was somehow at odds with things like "reaching one's potential," "getting ahead," and in the new-age parlance of my formative young adulthood, being "self-actualized." Oh dear!

Somehow, if one was content—and admitted it—one was just not getting it. No, contentment was reserved for brief, stolen moments until the process of getting on with the real work began again.

How did I miss that one might be content in and with that "real work"? That perhaps it was not an "either/or" proposition? Once in a great while, I met people who did not fall into the trap of believing one must suffer, struggle, or be quite serious in order to succeed on their given paths as artist, businessperson, social worker, or dairy farmer. But back then, they seemed to be few. And they always stood out to me. At the time, I couldn't have said why, exactly.

Harmony. Easiness. Enrichment. Play. In accor*dance* with. Practicing True Beauty is in large part about the pursuit and creation of harmony in all actions and interactions in our daily living. It is about putting the *arts* back into the concept of the "living arts."

Harmony infers twosome, a more-than-one-some—hence relationship! So a further aspect of my definition of True Beauty must be this: *beauty is harmonious relationships.*

Electromagnetism and the Definition of Beauty

The idea of beauty and attraction cannot be overlooked. Attraction has its roots in magnetism. Electromagnetism is a universal force. New discoveries are being made about the ubiquitous nature of the electromagnetism field virtually every day. There is attraction and its opposite, repulsion. That with which we resonate, we are drawn to, and we say we are attracted. That which creates discord in us we withdraw from—we might say we are repulsed. Do we characterize our response to the objects of these feelings as beautiful versus ugly?

So in further defining True Beauty, I would add that it is any "that" which inspires—inspires joy, appreciation, imitation, replication, and emergence. Beauty inspires and evokes a sense of connectedness, a sense, in short, of what theologians term the *eternal divine.*

But most interestingly, why? What is the nature and role—in fact, responsibility of—beauty? Is it a force in the universe? How is it that no matter where one goes on the planet, all human consciousness resonates with beauty? I believe *all* consciousness does. Beauty is definitely far more than skin deep.

Just to reiterate—in this book, we will not address beauty as it is considered when applied to the human form. That is an area of cultural taste in which many more worthy and clever than I have become mired. It is also the highly charged and politicized arena in which the trivialization of beauty has grossly blossomed, riding on the back of a rigid, static, and Hellenic cultural taste.

Everybody needs beauty as well as bread, places to play in and pray in, where nature may heal and give strength to body and soul.

–John Muir

Defining Ugly

And then there is beauty's opposite. What is meant by "ugly"? I will address it only briefly here to better clarify the broader parameters of True Beauty.

From the *Oxford American Dictionary, ugly* is defined as: "1. unpleasant to look at or to hear. 2. unpleasant in any way, hostile and threatening."

This is a rather superficial definition in my wordy-girl opinion. By that definition, the soup I ordered at dinner last night might be described as ugly, when really, it just didn't taste good *to me*—it had some weird unpleasant taste; perhaps too much cilantro?

Unpleasant equals *ugly?* I don't think so. Aren't there gradients in between? And of course, what is "unpleasant" to one isn't necessarily so to another. The soup referred to actually tasted quite good to the chef and others, I'm sure.

No. My definitions for ugly are quite a bit different. As with beauty, the concept of ugly has become misunderstood. Beauty is everywhere, and what we categorize as "ugly" may not really be so. It may merely be repulsive—unpleasant, unattractive, undesirable—to an individual. Does that make it truly ugly? And whether it is ugly, repulsive or not—it is usually also necessary. So we can say that ugly is in the eye of the beholder. Attitude and perception is everything.

I want to be clear here that there is an important place for destruction, as we will explore elsewhere along the Way of True Beauty. Entropy and destruction are parts of the sacred cycle of life, death, and resurrection. Entropy and erosion are part of *wabi-sabi,* a Japanese perception of beauty.

In my definition, something becomes ugly only when it is serving no purpose that is "of life," or when it is so out of sync with the cycle of life as to create overall imbalance. In our universe, there are attractors and there is repulsion. Ugly, like beauty, is a wavelength with which we resonate—or not. Our current cultural norms equate repulsion with the notion of ugly. Or, as one dictionary might have us believe, unpleasant.

I believe "common ugly" is that which we personally do not resonate with, and there is what I'll call "true ugly," which, defined below, is gratuitous, purposeless destruction and does not further the life-force.

Here are some definitions of ugly to consider before we go on. These are definitions that operate in the True Beauty ontology:

1. Ugly is that which intentionally suppresses the life-force.

2. Ugly is *gratuitous* destruction with no phoenix in sight.

3. Ugly is an energy that has only negative impact.

Beauty is not in the face;
beauty is a light in the heart.
—Kahlil Gibran

The Sociopolitical Implications

It has become appallingly obvious that our technology has exceeded our humanity.

—Albert Einstein

Global Awareness and Its Effect on the Collective Unconscious

When information and news was local, contained by geographic and technical boundaries, the impact of that news remained local—whether good or devastating. Neighbors helped; they celebrated or grieved with one another.

With the advent of technology and instant global communication, news of events can be known everywhere—its impact both visually and audibly transmitted and felt. The event's attendant "reality" is made more dense by the awareness, the thoughts replicated by all the thought-wave patterns emitted almost simultaneously by *all the watchers.* Not only our collective unconscious, but a collective *consciousness* is being formed and massed. This is a powerful force.

This is serious enough, if the situation stood as neutrally as that, if we all were left to receive the information and process it as individuals. But it doesn't and we aren't.

There are many "interpreters" of the world's events telling us what happened and what to think about it. The negative is highlighted and sensationalism is raised above worthiness. The media with its spin, as well as politicians, corporations, and advertisers, are all helping to create the effect that is being experienced by so many minds at once, felt in so many guts at once, resonating or repulsing in so many hearts—at once, *in the same moment.*

The lack of True Beauty shows up in our cultural tolerance of mediocrity and gratuitous ugliness. Again media is a major player here, as a prime and pervasive example being the way in which so much popular media celebrates sensationalism, enshrines the ugly as the norm (think gratuitous violence), perpetuating fear and a sense that we live in a constant state of heightened hostility.

In such a current environment, beauty has been reduced to appearance and relegated to only the surface of things—and beings. We have been conditioned to mistake glamour for beauty. Glamour is defined as "magic, enchantment" and having connotations of being a trick, not real. While there is nothing intrinsically wrong with magic or enchantment, they, like beauty, have fallen prey to misunderstanding and trivialization. And True Beauty is not a trick or illusion; it is very real and essential.

As the population has grown, so too have these societal control techniques using fear and intimidation. While we can always "turn off the tube" or shut down the screen, the truth is that most of us don't.

I work hard at being amazed rather than deeply offended at how our culture has evolved its mass media. And yes, *I fear* for the minds and hearts and souls of the children plugged into its toxic flow.

What *are* we creating?

Alternatively, what might we create?

What is and has been influencing our awareness of True Beauty?

Disassociation from True Beauty

How is it that we get separated from this True Beauty? How does it happen, and what replaces it?

One everyday example of our separation might be as common as our nutritional cycle. These days we are so disassociated from our food sources that children think chickens come from plastic boxes or buckets and spinach from a cellophane bag. What a shocking experience for a city kid to cut a wad of spinach from a plant or pull a carrot out of the earth, with dirt hanging from its orange self—and call each fresh and healthy! A quick wash and, *voila!*, ready to eat!

The distractions of our complex mode of modern-day living have helped distance us from those once natural connections to True Beauty. In our tech-savvy, mechanized, first-world countries, individuals are no longer directly dependent upon the natural world to survive. We have layers of intermediaries and corporate structure between our dinner plate, say, and the fish in the river or that carrot in the earth.

What *is* dirt? What is dirt-y? What *is* all that cement and blacktop? What is it covering up? What is ugly? What is beautiful?

Have our management and coping skills put too much stock in convenience and too little into consciousness?

A Word about "Taste"

And then there is the thorny issue of "taste." What is considered beautiful, or "tasteful," and what is not, or "taste*less*." The notion of taste has evolved to play a role, I think, in our disassociation from True Beauty.

I grew up with this idea of "having taste." In the context of True Beauty, it is a completely fabricated notion. It is based on a codified set of aesthetics that are developed to telegraph class and education, so as to better distinguish one and help find one's proper tribe members. Therefore, the concept of taste is worthy to bring to this discussion only as a good example of the breach that separates us from True Beauty.

Separation occurs when there is the Observer and the Observed. When the idea of taste transcends discernment for personal choice and becomes an ethos that defines a group—indeed *labels one as belonging to a certain class* or level of education—then it is a very effective tool of separation. A veritable crowbar crammed firmly between subject and object, "us" and "them." Most importantly, there is no room or recognition of the field of potential—in either group. Unity or the realization of an essential oneness doesn't have a chance.

Whole books have been written defending, attacking, and defining the notion of *taste* in aesthetics. Immanuel Kant, in his *Critique of Judgment* (1790), did a fine job elucidating the subjective and universal nuances in the judgment of aesthetics. David Hume went so far as to create standards for taste and "wrote the book," so to speak, in an essay in 1757. I am reminded again of the degree to which our understanding of beauty has become departmentalized, rationalized, and trivialized. Stolid. Static.

Hume's stance, in essence, is that taste is based on class, education, and experience. That through *educated* experience one learns judgment and discernment. True enough. In my ethos, this would be just fine if the discourse and its implications were strictly limited to the *individual* and the individual's own choices and not broadcast as a level of societal worthiness, acceptability—and beauty.

I take exception to shortcuts of perception, recipes—"standards of taste" that have in practice become "coda of beauty." While I can appreciate the probable intention behind this work, the resultant elitism and narrowing of aesthetics are consequences that have proved to be at least equally counterproductive.

The concept of taste as a definitor is the child of a civilization that has become so dependent upon appearance, the surfaces of perception, and comparative values, with little to no regard for intrinsic and/or deeper values that it can no longer rely on the honest and intuitive senses of its individuals.

Further, such standards can be a code to create and preserve a static and deadened place-holder, so there is mere repetition of "beauty" based on a long-ago discovery. The freshness of beauty no longer exists; discovery is not encouraged. Formulas are in place. Notice how this helps to preserve the status quo in a society.

While the beauty of that long-ago time still is, beauty just does not end there. We, here and now, have perceptions to be made and beauty to see, appreciate, and resonate with.

Whitehead summarizes well when he says, "These standards have served the Western races well. But…it is backward looking…Today the world is passing into a new stage of its existence…It is really not sufficient to direct attention to the best that has been said and done in the ancient world. The result is static, repressive, and promotes a decadent habit of mind." (*Adventures of Ideas.*)

Yes! Though written three-quarters of a century ago, it is as true today if not truer: "the world is passing into a new stage of its existence," and it is important that we not be hindered by old ideas or ideals that are not flexible enough to embrace new situations, new ideas, new needs.

Frankly, the issue of taste shouldn't be much more than a hiccup in the cosmology of True Beauty as defined herein. Beauty in our new operating paradigm is not concerned with rigid standards of taste, yet we must be aware of its place in our current societal psyche to more readily and easily embrace True Beauty.

It is the artists and inventors who are on consciousness's edges, the change makers and evolutionaries.

The Repression of Beauty

If it's important, someone or some entity will be threatened by it and try to stifle it. Beauty does not escape this unfortunate axiom.

What stops us as beings from naturally gravitating to beauty? Why do otherwise? What motivation is there? What gets between us and our ability to have joy, completeness, surprise, pleasure, wonder, awe, delight—the experience of beauty? Why wouldn't creating and perpetuating beauty be a guiding motivator in humankind's societal evolution? Why do we seem to have come to a place in our culture where we appear to actually repress beauty and be elevating its opposite?

Well, that is a long list of questions.

Perhaps one underlying cause is the evolution of cultural attitudes purporting that beauty is naïve; the belief that its pursuit is not difficult, nor complex. That beauty is about appearance and surfaces only—a glamour. Perhaps because beauty and its daughter, elegance, can be simple and conceived so simply, we think it must be unworthy.

True Beauty defies the "superficial" in all aspects: conversation, action, and environmental choices.

Other plausible reasons for the suppression of beauty trace back, inevitably, to those societal control issues.

The control and/or suppression of artists, creators, thinkers, and inventors is often a first step in managing a growing civilization. Beauty evokes a response and begs for replication, if just to further understand and be engaged more completely in beauty. Thus, it inspires education—and an educated population is a difficult one to police. Those on a learning path often travel to find teachers and other like-minded seekers; they see other ways of being and learn other ways of thinking.

The lack of True Beauty shows up in our cultural tolerance of mediocrity.

These seekers ask questions, challenge the status quo, and are fascinated by differences rather than intimidated by them. It is the artists and inventors who are on consciousness's edges, the change makers and evolutionaries. And these tendencies can be the seeds of revolutionaries. Oh yes, established order can frown upon such ones.

Another entire book could be written on the repression of True Beauty in today's culture and its resultant sociological and psychological pathologies. This current unpopularity of beauty beyond shallow appearance or sentimentalism exists and has been building for some time. You know those voices and their phrases: The beautiful is naïve, shallow, trite, or unsophisticated. Material things will increase happiness. Or, beauty is only skin deep—talking about the beauty that is about appearance only.

And those who mistake these glamours as True Beauty are like those hungry ones who eat bread made from sawdust—and then wonder why there is still a hollow, empty feeling in the pits of their stomachs.

The jaded, skeptical, and misguided attitudes shrouding True Beauty must end and cease to pollute our consciousness!

Sociopolitical Needs for True Beauty

We need to reclaim the power of True Beauty in our everyday lives. We need only look around or read the news to see why. I've found that many people, when I broach this subject, think I am a bit dim, naïve, or just oversimplifying. Anything but.

Our lack of awareness of beauty and its role in the natural rhythms of the world is the very thing that has brought on so many of the crises in which we now find ourselves. It is easier to see the correlation when looking at the environment, but the lack of True Beauty reaches far further. It's evident in every corrupt government, greedy business, and heartless administration of any organization. It is evident in the malaise born of anomie and the rise of our technology-addicted society.

Much of the deprivation and degradation that is so apparent in the world around us today is due to this systemic neglect and trivialization of beauty in the fullest sense of the concept. In today's various economies, too much consideration is given to return on investment (ROI), with "I" meaning only *monetary* investment. What about investment in environment, longevity, harmony, and serenity? And our *returns* on them?

When I consider synchronicity, ants, synergy, chocolate, living systems theory, laughter, chaos theory, bees, entropy, light, fractals, holograms, kelp beds, hyperspace, intuition, quantum physics, and the Rig Veda—to name only a few—this fabulous, diverse, and complex stew of stuff and concepts seems to serve up one conclusion for me: the perpetuation of beauty.

Unfortunately, in the majority of our public schools today, when budget time rolls around, the arts are the first thing to be cut from the curriculum—even before athletics. If we accept that exploring and making art is participation in the flow of True Beauty, then what has happened to the wisdom of our ancients who touted truth, beauty, and goodness as their three central tenets?

Thomas Moore, in *Care of the Soul,* said, "This assumption that beauty is an accessory, and dispensable, shows that we don't understand the importance of giving the soul what it needs. The soul is nurtured by beauty. What food is to the body, arresting, complex, and pleasing images are to the soul...

if we lack beauty in our lives, we will probably suffer familiar disturbances in the soul—depression, paranoia, meaninglessness, and addiction."

As a result, we end up with the psychopathologies that we see in our culture of temporariness, waste, disrespectfulness, entitlement, and anomie.

So, from this perspective, one importance of True Beauty is its integral role in maintaining a healthy soul: "If we are going to care for the soul…then we will have to understand beauty more deeply and give it a more prominent place in life." (Moore, *Care of the Soul.*)

Amen.

"We feel most alive in the presence of the Beautiful for it meets the needs of our soul," says poet John O'Donohue.

Who among us has not felt this experience?

So, if we must reinstate the importance of True Beauty in all things, intentions, and actions, and we must do so *now*—how? What are some possible actions we might take? The Beauty Practices help show the way.

But first, let's put all of this in the context of our universe. Yep! The universe!

A Bit about Science and Its Role

We humans have always reached for the divine.

DARK ENERGY, A substance of our universe not currently understood, is believed to constitute 68 percent of said universe, and dark matter 27 percent. Luminous matter, made up of photons, is the stuff we understand best and from which all matter is constructed—and it is a mere 5 percent. Only *5 percent* of the universe! (This is according to latest estimates from NASA.)

Luminous matter is what *we* are constructed of—humans, plants, rocks, animals, and our fluid, mineral earth. I heartily concur, then, with cosmologist Brian Swimme's statement: "matter is rare and precious."

How does this relate to the concept of True Beauty? In this way: isn't it interesting that in our current culture(s), we are learning—and have been learning—to *despise* matter. At best, we are conditioned to disrespect it and to take it for granted. Matter is crude. Matter is *stuff.* Matter is servant to us—material to be used, exploited. Matter is profane.

Really?

As David Korten so succinctly says, "The sacred became the servant of the profane." (*The Great Turning: From Empire to Earth Community.*)

This is evident in some religious, ecological, and political attitudes and cultural values all over the globe in one way or another. Think land use, energy-related issues, and air pollution to name just the usual suspects.

Attitudes toward flesh itself are revealing. We have sold and traded in human flesh. Female flesh is all about thinness in the current culture. Doesn't this communicate that the less body the better? The female body and its reproductive organs are still *things* to be owned, covered, and legislated.

Beyond human flesh, there is the abuse of other natural resources—whether animal flesh or plant beings—they are "objects" to be mass produced and used in service to our species-centric considerations. And in these times, I don't think I need to do more than mention the issue of the earth's mineral and oil deposits and the embattled relationships that have evolved around that form of matter.

Yet it is all *rare*, precious, luminous matter.

There is a prevailing and ubiquitous disregard of beauty and the sacredness of nature—Nature, the natural world, is the primary manifestation of matter in this time/space place we know as Earth, and it is such a very, very small percentage of our universe.

It is of further interest to consider that currently, a scientific theory posits that all matter "pops" into existence out of said dark energy and pops out of existence again. It is only what remains that becomes our "visible and tangible" world. One must wonder, since there is so much dark energy—that 68 percent of our universe—why is matter so rare? Why doesn't it manifest more, and more often? Or does it manifest, and it is just outside the realm of our current levels of understanding and perception?

While matter is an important form in which beauty can manifest, indeed the form in which we are most familiar recognizing beauty, it is not the only form. I suggest that True Beauty is a field and a resonance. This speaks to beauty's link to harmony. Some propose that the universe began with a sound. A single musical note, perhaps? More than one, and you might have a harmony—wavelengths that flow together in synchronicity. Wavelengths exist in a field.

Here is yet another definition of True Beauty: *Beauty is the synergistic, flowing field that holds all in dynamic, resonating harmony as the next movement unfurls.*

Our "hard sciences" of today seem to tell us only about relationships between measurements. Isn't this, really, all they boil down to? While instructive and a very handy tool, such science cannot be the definitive modality. Relationships between measurements tell us nothing essential about the *qualitative* nature of the "its" being measured.

I deeply resonate with Alfred North Whitehead, who puts forth the philosophy that science as it is currently practiced is basically deluded—the world isn't made of atoms, electrons, and so on. Instead, it is a never-ending process of aesthetic moments of choice, of feeling. He names this *prehensions* (a term he created), which he defines as moments that are constantly occurring, dispersing, perishing as the next occasion comes into being to repeat the never-ending cycle. Whitehead actually bases his vision of our world on aesthetics and treats physics as merely superstructure. Ha! I love that!

Yet while such process philosophy has become commonplace and accepted among many scientists, as a culture we still cling to our comfy practical/practiced viewpoint of a reality consisting of static, inanimate matter and separate energy and space. We have only to look at how the medical sciences are still practiced to realize how firmly this is entrenched.

Whether Plato, Whitehead, Isaac Newton, Oprah Winfrey, Jonas Salk, Gautama Buddha, Van Gogh, Deepak Chopra, Stephen Hawking, or our next door neighbor it is out of our strong human aspiration to divinity that we ask, inquire, search, explore, and—yes—measure. We humans are curious; we are driven.

In our scientific searching, we come up with some data, we spin possible stories about the interesting measurements and their relationships to one another. Some of the stories are even probable, and they gain adherents and popularity. So we elevate them, and they become "theory." And sometimes, when a theory gains great popularity, we name it "the truth." We do this because we are struggling to *understand.* The wondrous human spirit wants to comprehend and fabricate a coherent whole out of the fragmentation that we are able to apprehend.

We are, in short, reaching for what many name the *divine.*

These processes of our inquiry are the means by which we engage, touch, tap into, and, yes, *play with* the divine. Our sciences are fine tools; it is just sad that we have, to such a great degree, forgotten about all the other toys and tools in our collective and figurative toolboxes: sensing, perceiving, intuiting, feeling, reflecting, emoting, engaging, and replicating to name a few.

It is all about *mystery.* We don't really know, except what we intuitively know, with our hearts. Or, as we will see later, we "gnow."

The Christian Bible says, "In the beginning was the Word," or a single musical note...a harmonic vibration. I add that it was a note of beauty.

As is the inner, so is the outer;
as is the great, so is the small;
as it is above, so it is below;
there is but One Life and Law:
and he that worth it is One.
Nothing is inner, nothing is outer;
nothing is great, nothing is small;
nothing is high, nothing is low,
in the Divine Economy.

—Hermetic Axiom

Natural Beauty

For the world is not painted or adorned,
but is from the beginning beautiful;
and God has not made some beautiful things,
but Beauty is the creator of the universe.

—Ralph Waldo Emerson

The natural world is often our first introduction to and relationship with external beauty—beauty without. And in our current urban-central, agribusiness culture, most people are only on a "nodding basis" with such beauty. While gardening is a giant industry and ranked a top hobby of American households, it is also true that too few souls participate in too little of nature's wild, uncontained beauty.

The importance of the natural world is beginning to reenter our modern consciousness. Its healing nature is being noted in some books, articles, and practices. The Japanese have evolved a practice called *shinrin-yoku,* or *forest bathing,* wherein one goes for a leisurely stroll through a forest for the health benefits. These benefits include the following:

- increased immune-system efficiency
- decreased blood pressure
- reduced stress
- reduced anxiety
- improved mood

And these are not all the reported benefits. We are beginning to wake up to the fact that distancing ourselves from the natural world is harmful. We are beginning to discover that spending time in and with the natural world heals us.

I believe it is in large part the natural world's eternal beauty, True Beauty, that heals, balances, and harmonizes. We are a part of the natural world. We resonate with it and feel best when we are synchronized with it.

So get thee to a garden! And a forest!

And remember when you are in a garden that aside from the obvious simple beauty that a garden creates, the relationships one forms while creating and tending it—with the soil, the plant, the visiting animals, birds, bees and insects, the weather—are enriching and enhancing—and sometimes annoying and frustrating.

Let's list that aspect under character development.

Some small but powerful practices we'll explore later that help reintroduce us to the rhythms of beauty might include turning off (or getting rid of) the TV, skipping the daily news from the fear-mongering mass media, or making dinner for a friend once a week or so. Sitting quietly each day (preferably outside) also ranks right up there.

A Bit of History

History teaches everything including the future.

-- Lamartine

The ancient Greeks thought a great deal about beauty, and modern philosophers and scientists have been building on their thoughts ever since. But it seems to me that for the past century, at the very least, we have not been elaborating and expanding upon Plato and his cohorts as they spoke about beauty; rather, we've gotten stuck on a few simplistic dogmas. Dumbing down, not delving into. In fact, Plato and other early philosophers found the subject of beauty so complex that they offered no straightforward definition of beauty.

And we haven't picked up on the challenge. We have been content with the inherited Greco-Roman standards of beauty. We have devolved into ideas of cute, pretty, and glamorous without bothering to look much deeper. Behaviorally, we have forgotten about beauty beyond appearances almost altogether.

Beauty is part of a time-honored trinity. Plato articulates the importance of truth, beauty, and goodness, and many succeeding philosophers have used these three legs of the stool of philosophical wisdom-truths upon which to build their work.

In fact, beauty is often viewed as superseding truth and goodness. Alfred North Whitehead states unequivocally, "Beauty is a wider, and more fundamental notion than Truth." And then he goes on to say, "Truth matters because of Beauty."

Indeed, the aestheticism movement in Europe and America in the nineteenth century caused quite a stir. One definition has it as "the belief that the pursuit of beauty is the most important goal, and that it is the artist's duty to orchestrate...elements from nature into a composition that... exists for its own sake, without regard to moral or didactic issues." (ArtLex.com, 2007.)

There are some constants in True Beauty that transcend every culture, persevere through every version of man's suppression of himself—culturally or personally—and his own inner knowingness: the light as it strikes the earth or a body of water; fresh fruits on the table; the sound of a loved one's laugh or of bird song; and the sense of coming home or a safe haven.

Like laughter or a smile, True Beauty is recognized, experienced, and known all over the globe. Let us once again acknowledge its importance. By taking up the challenge and moving beyond our inherited understanding of beauty, we can make history that future historians will be teaching from for centuries.

Beauty and Creativity

Creativity is the actualization of potentiality, and…
the process of creation is the form
of unity of the Universe.

—Alfred North Whitehead, *Adventures of Ideas*

To make art, as a fine artist or as a handcrafter, to have an idea or vision and then bring it into combinations of luminous matter, however one does it—through paper, paint, wood, cloth, plant, sound, or metal—is to interpret and create. It is in the *process* of creation that we can experience True Beauty. The process itself is a direct way to enter into the flow of the universe and the life-force itself.

The flow of creativity is the flow of the universe, its wavelength. To create anything is to be "in the flow." By its very nature, one of creativity's intrinsic outcomes must be beauty. Because *despite the product,* or its merits, it is the process of being creative that is in itself a practice of True Beauty, an experience of the divine to be had by all. Priest, social psychologist, and prolific writer Diarmuid O'Murchu frames it this way: "The creative process itself—with its beauty and elegance, but also with its pain and destructibility—is our primary, tangible source for experiencing the divine energy." (O'Murchu, *Quantum Theology.*)

There are many books and writings about creativity, but not so many about beauty. I found it interesting, and not a little

Art is the human recognition and expression of beauty, a manifestation of our need to replicate it.

disturbing, that in all the references I studied over the years, it is very rare to find "beauty" indexed other than in relation to makeup, diet regimes, or supermodels. I had more success searching under "aesthetics," and then it was in rather arcane philosophy books. Unless one is investigating cosmetics, it seems beauty is not a concept worthy of referencing. This needs to be changed in the culture. It needs to be right in there in our discourses with, say, archetypes, bulimia, and catechism, with video games, indigo children, identity theft, and immortality. How has beauty, as a driving force in our psyches, our ontology, been so forgotten? *So* trivialized?

Whew! It's time to go for a beauty break.

Beauty versus Art

What is the relationship between art and beauty? Wonderfully, it is a couple of guys writing about chaos theory that put it best, I think. In their book, *Seven Life Lessons of Chaos,* John Briggs and David Peat state: "Nature makes its fractal forms out of matter and energy. The material of art includes human consciousness, as well."

Art is the human recognition and expression of beauty, a manifestation of our need to replicate it. I use the term *art* to refer to the man-made variety, in order to stay out of the thorny peripheral issues concerned with "what constitutes art" (which is another purview altogether). We will accept the idea that art exists in nature, but let's make a distinction here between man-made art versus nature's creation. I use *creation* to mean all that *is,* both seen and unseen by the human eye arising from the organism we think of as the universe—our earth, sun, the skies, neutrinos, space, bosons—*everything*-- The Isness.

It is important to note that often nature, creation, is many people's first and most direct sensate experience of the beautiful: a glimpse of the sky, trees, clouds, or sunlight; the sound of birdsong or rain on a windowpane; the sight of small, green, growing things; and the smell of soil.

Art is humankind participating in this process of creation—adding, mixing it up, interfering in wonderful and sometimes whimsical ways—adding human consciousness and consideration to the Isness. But by my lights, it is with a sense, an underlying purpose, consciously or unconsciously, to replicate the True Beauty—either through direct replication or through contrast and complement.

I make art. But my artwork itself is *not* True Beauty. It is, however, in my *process of making* art that I *experience* True Beauty. When assembling a sculpture or adding pencil work to a monoprint (the medium doesn't matter) and I get into the flow of creating, making—*that* is experiencing True Beauty. The outcome, the piece of "art," is the by-product of that experience.

Humility in the artist is his frank
acceptance of all experiences,
just as Love in the artist is simply that sense of Beauty
that reveals to the world its body and its soul.
—Oscar Wilde

To Gnow

Intuition will tell the thinking mind where to look next.
—Jonas Salk, MD

We live in the Age of Reason, Logic, and Science. I say the *Dark* Age of Reason and Science as it disallows most other ways of knowing, specifically, "gnowing," and that is not a typo.

"To know" has come to reference an existing fact, one generally accepted. Interestingly, this was not always the case. The word has several etymological origins (Greek, Teutonic, romantic) and therefore carries differing connotations. Specifically, it has meant to know *with the mind,* though earlier on it also included to know with the senses. But this last has been eclipsed by the former. In our modern times, for something to be knowable, it must be of mind and matter: quantifiable and visible as in, "if I can't see it, it doesn't exist!" It seems to *know* something these days, there must be a study or a poll or a proof!

Right? Wrong.

Many indigenous cultures take for granted the existence of an inner knowing, that there are many individual truths and levels of knowingness. But that word, *know,* just did not seem to do justice to describing the experience of gaining and retaining information that shamans, psychics, diviners, and some regular ol' people were receiving. The word *intuition* is hardly taken seriously. So *to gnow* or *gnowing* is a term I use to describe discerning, observing, or garnering information. You won't find it in any dictionary. Not yet, anyway.

How did this term come about? I didn't make it up—at least, not by myself. It was a group *aha!* moment.

A Story

It was 2007, and I had signed up for a class with one of my New Universe Story heroes, cosmologist Brian Swimme. In fact, taking this class was one of my justifications for renting a house outside San Francisco for the year. Escaping another Vermont winter was the other one.

The class was a private one, not under the auspices of any educational institution, and was by invitation. I was very excited to be a part of it. In a real nutshell, it was a sort of beta class on integrating some of the implications of Thomas Berry's *The New Story* and the emerging paradigm shift into our life choices. At least, that is what I was expecting.

On the appointed day, I drove into San Francisco, an adventure all of itself, as I did not know the city well, and, since I'd learned to drive in Vermont, I had little big-city driving experience. But I got there, found the building on the street that ran along Golden Gate Park, and headed in.

There were about forty or so people there. I knew no one. We introduced ourselves and learned that the class would be a lecture in the morning and some sort of related activity in the afternoons, usually outdoors. Sounded great.

The class met every other week, and while the first couple of classes started out well, as the program progressed, I realized that it was not at all what I had been expecting. I was becoming increasingly uncomfortable as my efforts to be open to this (surprising) experience kept failing.

By now, I was remembering a few of my classmates' names. One day during the lunch break, some of us found ourselves in the same nearby café. Sitting together, our normally casual conversation turned into a critique of the course so far. It quickly became evident that I was not the only one who had been hoping for something different.

A few of us left the café together to get back to the classroom early: Laura, Sophie, Bridget, and I. Laura, in her lovely flowing scarves and long skirt, tripped on an edge of sidewalk that had been thrust upward by a tree root. ("Ah!" I thought later. "It was the universe conspiring with us!") She went down hard. We gasped and gathered round her as you might imagine. We determined that no limb was broken, but an ankle was twisted, a shoe strap broken, and her forehead had an ugly and bloody scrape.

We helped Laura back to our classroom where we found Louise and Sylvia, friends who habitually brought their own very healthy lunches with them, speaking with Alice, another student. They rushed to our aid, and we all made much of Laura, finding pillows and Band-Aids, making her comfortable, and embellishing on the tale of that wicked and inconvenient sidewalk.

That afternoon's class activity was supposed to be rowing boats on the pond in Golden Gate Park. Laura couldn't go and I did not want to, so I offered to stay with her. So did the others. So there we were, fledgling mutineers: me, Laura, Sylvia, Louise, Alice, Sophie, and Bridget (not real names, of course, for privacy's sake).

We spent a lovely afternoon in our empty classroom, getting to know one another; discussing the ecology of Golden

Gate Park, spirit worlds, and electromagnetic fields (Sophie was writing an article about them); discovering that Laura was from LA and a witch…the usual women's chitchat!

We agreed to meet outside the class to independently pursue some of the topics we had been hoping to cover in the course. At least, that's how it began.

Over the next several weeks, one by one, we each quit the class. We came to call ourselves the "Cosmic Boat Women" because we'd jumped the class ship and struck out on our own.

It was the beginning of a long and deeply influential set of relationships.

We had long discussions about magic, the sacred, how the sacred manifests in other cultures, the uses of reason and logic, the misuses of reason and logic, knowing, instinct, spiritual guides, feminine wisdom…feminine knowing. And we had experiences. Shamanic journeys. Treks up mountains to beautiful and sacred places. Altar and ritual making. Quiet listening to the wild in the wild.

Several of these women used a term I hadn't heard before: *gyns.* Well, I *had* been sheltered in the world of business. I ascertained that "gyns" took the place of girls/gals. (Gyns vs. guys I wondered? A California feminist thing I wondered? I just plain wondered a lot in the Cosmic Boat Women—a good thing.)

Then, during one of our gatherings, we were discussing ways of knowing, intuiting, sensing—all the ways we knew there to be of receiving, sending, and processing information. One of these ways, relegated now to the annals of esoteric ancient Christian theology, is gnosis, a (feminine!) Greek noun meaning knowledge attained through spiritual enlightenment or mystical means.

Our conversation that day led us to the conviction that the feminine intuitive way of knowing, one that is often informed by the unseen world, such a knowing-sensing, should have its own word, different from the overworked "to know." With tips of our collective hat to the whimsy of gyns, the wisdom of the Gnostics, and the irony of homophones…out it came: the term *to gnow* was born.

It should be in the lexicon. So here it be.

By the way, the Cosmic Boat Women met for years, long after I moved from California. So that beta course from Brian Swimme, though short lived for members of the Cosmic Boat Women, had life-changing influences on us all.

> *Gnosis is not primarily rational knowledge. The Greek language distinguishes between scientific or reflective knowledge ("He knows mathematics") and knowing through observation or experience ("He knows me"). As the Gnostics use the term, we could translate it as "insight," for Gnosis involves an intuitive process of knowing oneself. Yet to know oneself, at the deepest level is to know God; this is the secret of Gnosis.*
>
> —Elaine Pagels, *The Gnostic Gospels*

From Cosmetology to Cosmology

TRUE BEAUTY IS a paradox that is far more complex—and simple—than (dare I say?) meets the eye. Most significantly, healing our relationship to beauty will in turn heal much of the pathology that our culture is currently suffering. When talking about *this* beauty, we are talking *cosmology*, not *cosmetology*. A seminal fact in why reclaiming True Beauty is so important.

Cosmology, from the Greek, originally meant "to order the universe." The term has evolved and broadened to reference the order and deep inner workings, relationships, and patterns of almost any system. I attended a conference on "The Cosmology of Health," for instance, that had speakers from every aspect of the health field – not only medical practitioners, but social services, lab techs, researchers, patients and their families. The cosmos of the health industry.

So when we address the cosmology of beauty, we are observing all its aspects, influences, and relationships. The patterns of True Beauty are everywhere, once we start noticing. Mathematicians, physicians, philosophers, physicists, and artists document the beautiful patterns that abound in our universe. One of my favorite sites to go view some surprising True Beauty is the NASA Hubble Telescope images.

This all-pervasive, powerful aesthetic force is integral to the health and balance of our cosmos. *Why*? Why is beauty the big thing? The skeptic may ask, "Wouldn't it make more sense to help out the planet if we just stop making wars, stop all the conflicts that seem to spring up like toxic mushrooms all over the globe?"

There will always be conflicts. The challenge is to *evolve* to a place where conflicts are resolved without violence, without warring. I don't know that reclaiming and restoring True Beauty to a more prominent place in human consciousness will entirely quell our human propensity to go to war. But I do know, and *gnow*, that if we are able to engage with True Beauty, it will influence conflict resolution a great deal for the positive. And most importantly, practicing True Beauty is something that we each can do, individually, to make this difference.

Timeliness is a factor here. The concept of beauty's essential centrality and importance is not new. Previous civilizations' tenets have revolved around beauty. What *is* new is the current urgency for this reinstatement. Although the core and universal nature of aesthetics has been promulgated in the past, it is critical to bring beauty forward—this time into *global consciousness*—as an integral guiding principal with its power to unite and heal. We have only to look around our crumbling institutions and old patterns to see that this is so.

How did we get to the point we are at today in our modern Western civilization? How did greed, corruption, and selfishness become so prevalent? How did our lives get so busy, our frustrations so many, and our sense of contentment and achievement so hard won?

Each individual practicing True Beauty can create cultural change.

We live in an atmosphere charged with the expectancy of change. Some culture watchers, cosmologists, and theologians believe the era in which we are living *needs* to be the period for forging a whole new paradigm, that the old operational ideas have outlived their usefulness, *en masse,* and are now just causing harm. Evidence of this is becoming increasingly apparent.

The shifting consciousness around humanity's place on the planet and our use of its resources is a prime example of this shift. Certainly, there have been recent events that support this hypothesis.

When people talk about "shifting the paradigm," it means changing the standard operating procedure as it relates to those cultural norms that have evolved. It means challenging our own expectations. It means creating a new, positive, and truly beautiful new normal.

It is exciting that anyone can contribute to this aspect of the shift work through independent, personal action. *Each individual can make significant changes in our cultural dynamics.* We can create cultural change through personal responsibility that manifests in our actions. It is the old "pebble in the water creating ripples" strategy. Or the butterfly wing/hurricane creation effect. Moving beauty out of the abstract and back into the realm of the concrete and actionable—*doable*—is key to a successful cultural and values shift.

To this end, I propose evolving a twenty-first-century applied philosophy of beauty: The Way of Beauty and its practices. Yes, *practices,* because True Beauty behaves as a verb as well. To reclaim beauty we must *do* it. The Way of Beauty shows us how. To have a positive impact, we must pursue True Beauty as action.

We must move from giving only lip service born of abstract philosophical theory (truth, beauty, and goodness) into behavioral practices born of value shifts based in this new, emergent paradigm.

And, here's how…

True Beauty is about cosmology, not cosmetology.

Part Two

The Way of True Beauty

Practicing True Beauty first requires cultivating the ability to turn off our "automatic pilot."

The True Beauty Practices

Bring beauty in, flow beauty out.

What Is Practicing Beauty?

WHAT IS A "practice"? How is it different from a habit or a daily routine? The difference lies in awareness and intent. What we name a *practice* for ourselves is a consciously chosen habit, a (sometimes) ritualized doingness that is purposefully elevated from other daily doings to honor the specific intent behind it. Implied in the term *practice* is an intent to progress forward or deeper. This meaning is not intrinsically implied in mere *habit.*

Practicing True Beauty is committing to an ongoing and progressive awareness of beauty. It is cultivating the ability to choose a state of awareness that overrides or turns off that comfy awareness level, which I call our *automatic pilot.*

You know about automatic pilot: it is that mental state that allows you to get to work without ever having to actually think about your route or to make coffee in the morning while your mind is busy planning the day ahead...it is the "shorthand" of perceiving, doing, and communicating.

The primary purpose of a beauty practice is to:

1. Turn off the shorthand of our sensing and perceiving abilities and turn on our more basic (yet often obscured) capabilities to sense and understand

2. Truly see and appreciate the harmonious and serendipitous relationships all around us

3. Create, cultivate, and nurture such wherever and however we are each individually able to do so

Practicing beauty is retraining the eye and the brain to avoid oversimplifying generalizations and isolating fragmentation, to see with the heart and the soul and to invigorate our natural capacity for wonder.

This perception and recognition of *True* Beauty is available to virtually everyone. As Helen Keller famously noted, "The best and most beautiful things in the world cannot be seen or even touched—they must be felt with the heart."

The Way of Beauty is this: to consciously pursue and cultivate beauty beyond surfaces and appearances, to recognize and honor its presence as well as actively engage in beauty's creation, and to preserve and return its prominence in our global culture. Indeed, practicing beauty as presented in these practices is to be in synchronicity with the healing of our planet and the physical and spiritual evolution of our universe and its inhabitants.

Beauty as Action

How can we *be* beauty? Well, easy: by our actions, we are known.

Through the beauty practices, we can evolve and expand our consciousness and not only survive but be productive, elegant, and facilitative elements in the universe as it proceeds in the continual birthing of its ever-expanding self.

Even though we are not perfect or 100 percent beautiful (and you know I'm not talking about the tabloid-magazine version), we can still strive to *be* beauty. True Beauty. We can strive to add harmony rather than discord into the energy of our personal universe(s) and therefore the universe itself. But this takes practice. Hence, the beauty practices. They help. They guide. They inspire.

1. Practice Seeing

It is one of the commonest of mistakes to consider that
the limit of our power of perception
is also the limit of all there is to perceive.
—Charles W. Leadbeater

Beauty is everywhere, if we only have eyes to see it and souls that wish to communicate it, and if we only stop using the shorthand of seeing and instead choose to *really* see. If we did so, we would not stop. We would become addicted to beauty. There's a great idea!

A Story

In the early 1990s, I was in California for a seminar. One morning, I was jogging leisurely through the hills of West Hollywood with Ian, an acquaintance from the classroom. I'd only recently arrived from Vermont's white and gray winter palette, and I was stunned by the lushness of southern California's version of February.

"Look at all the greens!" I exclaimed to Ian as we wound up the path through Griffith Park.

Ian was in the music industry, an elderly Brit who managed rock-and-roll bands (some that I'd heard of, so I was impressed). I figured this was a relatively innocuous comment to make as we huffed and puffed our way up a slow grade.

He looked at me, one eyebrow raised, and asked, "Whatever do you mean? *Greens?*"

I was surprised by his question.

"Well, look at that yellowy-green tree over there; it's almost fluorescent! It practically leaps out at you. Just look how bright it is! Especially against that line of dark, blackish evergreens behind it," I gushed and stopped jogging, pointing straight up. "See? And look at the sparkly, emerald-green foliage just above us."

Ian stood beside me, glad for a break, and looked up. His nose was all scrunched up, his mouth open, and brow furrowed. I couldn't tell if it was the exertion of the run or confusion about my color commentary. Or perhaps it was a bit of both. We walked for a bit, giving me a chance to catch my breath... and continue.

"See all the different hues of green up there on the hill? See when they are all clustered together how different they look against one another? The grays of the eucalyptus, those bluey greens, that silly giant palm sticking up in the middle of it all. See? See?"

I think I went on and on. It had been a long Vermont winter, and my eyes were hungry for colors other than gray. They feasted on all the colors, cataloging every green hue the scenery offered up. Purple green, lime green, brown green, emerald green, blue green, black green, grays that were green, greens that were gray.

Ian laughed and then said in his handsome British accent, "I never noticed it before. I just thought of it all as, well...green."

I never saw Ian again after spending those intense few weeks together at the seminar. But about a year later, I received a small note card in the mail. On the cover was a lovely artist's watercolor of a forest. Written on the inside was:

Lisa,
Wanted to let you know. On our run that morning in LA
you opened my eyes by showing me all the greens.
Thank you for teaching me how to truly see.
Love, Ian.

That note made my week. My month. I had been able to share the gift of seeing with someone.

The Importance of the Practice

"Seeing," as I am using it here, is really a metaphor for all sensings, both of the physical and of the intuitive sorts. Opening up to our visual capabilities is a great place to start honing all perceptions. Yet our eyesight is only one way into the universe of perception. Indeed, perception is not dependent upon only our physical senses but our *intuitive* senses as well.

Too often, we are on autopilot. We are not really aware of our surroundings. We are not truly seeing, sensing, being in *relationship* with our immediate environments and the stimuli that is coming into our selves (not to mention what we are putting out). This was the case for Ian.

Autopilot, our shortcut method, has its advantages, of course. It is a necessary approach to use at times when speed and efficiency are deemed the most important qualities and outcomes in a task or an encounter. But when that's not the case?

Too often, being on autopilot is not a conscious choice; we are simply *on* it. Our brains register—"Green. I know what that is."—and we see no further. As a result, we end up missing much—all the nuances are lost. We are not really conscious; we are not aware and truly in the moment.

Green is just a shorthand label for a zillion different energy waves playing with light, another zillion wavicles that produce effects we have named green, *verte, verde.* We can choose to engage and really look at *green* and see it for all the different vibrations/colors it really is.

Or look at someone's face, perhaps a familiar one. Imagine seeing it for the first time. Or look into that person's eyes; can you see a soul in there? Take a walk in your neighborhood. Can you see anew the street, a storefront? Or that weird contraption called a *grocery cart?*

Feel someone else's confusion or joy. Can you? Or sense the feel of a place—the entry hall in an apartment building, a wooded area along a trail, a busy city corner. These are all ways of seeing that incorporate not only our eyes but many other senses as well.

As we reach out and into these "others," we begin creating *relationships.* Being in relationship is an intrinsic element in the way of True Beauty, in understanding that True Beauty is active. Engaging in and with this sort of beauty is in part recognizing our participation in myriad relationships. We will explore the nature of relationships a great deal as we go forward.

For me, truly seeing/sensing is like Alice's rabbit hole. Once you go down it the first time, nothing seems the same anymore.

Practice seeing. You'll find the habit goes far beyond the merely visual.

To Practice Really Seeing

1. Challenge your own assumptions. What *aren't* you noticing? For Ian it was color. To see/sense something is to feel and notice it. It may be helpful to know that the process of seeing and sensing does not necessarily include the act of evaluating that which is being sensed.
    a. Play the "what color is..." game with yourself or your family. What color is the grass in the field? What color are the windows in that building? What color is a raindrop?
    b. Notice what you *don't* notice. For instance, can you recall the building on the first corner you pass every morning? How many stories is it? What color is the inside of the shoes you're wearing right now? What does the handle of your hairbrush feel like? Start to notice those things that are on continual automatic pilot. You don't have to take them all off autopilot; just be conscious of the choice to, say, not feel the texture of your hairbrush handle. You get the idea.
    c. Open up your receivers—skin, eyes, nose, intuition, ears—and practice *see*ing with all of them. *Sense* both your external and internal environments. Turn off your automatic pilot.

2. What comes to your attention once you have opened up and increased your seeing/sensing? What comes to your attention *repeatedly*? Colors? Textures? People? Their faces? The taste of food? Architecture? The list of possibilities is endless. But whatever you're most

noticing, pay attention! What you're seeing is that which attracts you!

When I say to pay attention, I am asking you to involve what attracts you in your life more. When you are involved with it more, you have the opportunity to study it. Be with and around it. (The word *study* sounds so stuffy. I don't mean the action to be so.) For instance, I love the natural world, I love color, and I love sunshine—so I have flower gardens. I am also fascinated with light, so paying attention to how the sunlight comes inside, I hang crystals in my windows that throw fabulous colorful prisms around my rooms.

So, some ways to do this studying aside from the "go-to-school" ways include the following:

a. When you are attracted to something—like science shows, sunlight, leatherwork, or animal husbandry—give yourself permission to pay more attention and involve it more into your life. Find others who are also interested in the subject, buy a book on the subject matter, write about it in your journal—take a class, even!
b. Don't listen to that little voice in there that says, "But you don't know anything about [fill in the blank]!"
c. Do listen to your gut about ways to spend your time. One day is different from the next!
d. Turn off the TV. While it can be a way to engage and learn, too often it is not and is used as an opiate. It really is not a relationship, much as it may feel like one. Minimize other sorts of screen time. Use computers and phones for *productivity*, not *opt-outivity*.

e. Read more, if you like that form. Make time to enjoy it. Consider including dictionaries and maps.

When one is engaged in/with what one loves, it is being "in the flow," a phenomenon that artists and artisans are familiar with. Time seems to stand still. Lunch- and dinnertimes come and go, and we are still weeding the garden, painting the canvas, repairing the engine, delving into the equation…that is being in the flow. It is a sacred place. And it need not be scarce.

Consistently practicing seeing plays a great part in derailing our automatic pilot. Really, that is what these practices help to do: live mindfully, intentionally, "beauty-fully."

Learning to truly see is the first essential step in noticing, nurturing, and becoming a part of all the True Beauty around and available to us all the time.

Evaluation—that is, judgment—need not be a part of the Seeing Practice in its first stages except as it relates to our safety. Evaluation can come eventually, in the form of discernment, noticing that which resonates with you personally, most deeply, and choosing to pay attention—and study it.

Heighten your awareness. Keep on becoming. It is important to pay attention to that which attracts you, to notice and learn. It is nurturing and validating your bit of the universe.

I believe noticing what you see and rolling it around in your brain is actually a form of creation—its preparation and precursor. Yet this all-important stage in the practice of seeing is one that is often overlooked or believed to belong only in the canons of childhood, something to be outgrown.

There has been a sense in our culture today that we are to "grow up" and "become" something...and then be done. Static. While currently this attitude is becoming less so—which I believe a good thing, as stasis is antithetical to the Way of Beauty and to nourishing our souls—it is still far too deeply ingrained. We must continue to sense then *study* that which attracts us in order to continue evolving and becoming...our most authentic and happy selves!

11. Practice Cultivating Awe

The most beautiful thing we can
experience is the mysterious.
It is the source of all true art and all science.
He to whom this emotion is a stranger,
who can no longer pause to wonder
and stand rapt in awe,
is as good as dead: his eyes are closed.
—Albert Einstein

Awe is a form of wonder that also holds a connotation of reverence for that which is being contemplated, for that which is a wonder. Delight and fear will sometimes accompany awe in a strange-yet-pleasant concoction.

Awe is preceded by wonder, often by a surprise. Life and living are full of surprises. There are many clichéd axioms about surprise; "expect the unexpected" or "life is what happens while you are making other plans" are two that immediately come to mind.

We are surprised by the unexpected, whether pleasant or unpleasant: a job change, a sudden weather shift, an inheritance, or a betrayal. While there is an element of surprise to awe, it is beyond mere surprise. To be in awe is to be in a particular, magical state of wonderment that has the potential to transform.

To cultivate awe is to open oneself up to True Beauty.

Awe does not necessarily have any connotation of evaluation with it. Aren't amazement and wonder fairly neutral states at first? A judgment response, if it comes, is secondary—is it a good surprise or a bad surprise? Are we delighted or disgusted?

A Story

Years ago, the late Dr. David Simon, author and cofounder of the Chopra Center for Well-Being, said something that struck me and has served me well in many situations. I was participating in a weeklong meditation retreat he co-led, an eye- and soul-opening experience. On this particular day, a conversation was brewing among the group bemoaning our perpetual state of war, the unfairness of bad things happening to good people, and so on. The whiny, complaining tone of the group was deepening. Dr. Simon suddenly interrupted the flow and rather forcefully said, "Look, shit happens; it always does. Shit always will happen. And when it does, you can choose to be offended by it, or you can choose to be amazed by it."

I was stunned. I thought about this statement for a moment and then laughed out loud. *So true!* I realized that in that nanosecond before I fell into being furiously offended by something or someone, really what I am is...shocked and amazed! In wonder! I have found myself...yes, in *awe* of a particular set of circumstances. I could be pissed off at a person who had so offended me with his/her incredibly stupid and inconsiderate action(s), or I could just be, stay, in amazement—in awe of such a different way of being, behaving, experiencing the world. It was a game-changing concept.

When we are surprised by something, confronted by a behavior or sight that is new or strange, there is no automatic pilot response available. Thus startled we have a more immediate, perhaps more authentic, ability to respond.

Now take that experience one step further: when confronted with something that is habitually or culturally interpreted as offensive, try staying simply amazed at such a thing! After all, to you, it *is* amazing, is it not? Try replacing moving to the probable negative judgmental step that often accompanies the new and unexpected with sustaining simple wonder and amazement at such a different object/behavior/circumstance. This is quite a game and can be challenging—from the prosaics of poop to the embeddedness of bigotry.

Imagine this: you are driving down the freeway at about seventy-two miles an hour in a sixty-five-mile-per-hour zone. A driver roars up from behind you, passes on the right, and cuts into your lane, pulling right in front of your vehicle. Then he slows down to fifty-five miles per hour. What is anyone's reaction? We yell, maybe swear, and hit the brakes! We are also shocked and taken by surprise.

From all the research publicized over the past few years, you probably know that your body—your cells, heart, nervous system—all respond to your emotional state. So when we blow up and swear at the road warrior who behaved so rudely, the only person we are harming is ourselves. Choosing to remain amazed at the other driver rather than descend into anger changes every cell in your body, altering the entire experience.

Amazement is about wonder and awe after the initial surprise—what I think of as light and curiosity. I imagine my eyes widening, brows lifting, and mouth opening in an "O" in awe of his action as the guy speeds by me. I know I would be curious about his reasons for speeding and then slowing down. Then I notice his funny bumper sticker that reads, "Stay Calm and Drive On." The irony of it makes me grin; I'll probably tell this story at dinner.

Offense is about anger, disregard, defensiveness, and perhaps a soupçon of dislike—all of which conspires to perpetrate "otherness." If I hadn't been endeavoring to practice beauty, I imagine my cells would have curdled, my heart would have thumped away erratically, and sweat might even have broken out on my forehead as my fists clutched the steering wheel—my whole body tense. The guy in the car ahead is not a person—he's an idiot, a jerk...a long list of epithets that I would never consider to be *me.* The guy is not like me, he's *other.* And I'm feeling no harmony here.

When home, I would have ranted about the crazy driver who almost killed everyone on the highway. And my audience would relate, telling me their horror stories of accidents...and the toxicity spreads.

While this beauty practice is not easy, especially at first, I find this to be a truly viable and often useful alternative to my former learned knee-jerk reaction of offense or defense (or both). Actually what will often happen for me still is that I must pull myself back into astonishment as I feel myself sliding into the annoyance/outrage/negative emotion that wants to take command. I return to my amazement. I keep my heart, cells, and nervous system on an even keel. I try to *see* "Mr. Road Warrior."

To practice beauty is to practice bringing the harmonious and the synergistic into our beings and our actions as much as possible—to cultivate being in awe of a difference rather than falling prey to offense, threat, and the resulting anger.

Here is what can be learned from Dr. Simon's statement: when amazement is our natural, immediate response, we often do not need to take that second, evaluative step. When we start to respond to a person or situation by being offended in some way, we can choose to nip that evaluative response before it begins and stay in simple amazement. If the surprising event warrants it, our amazement may even grow into awe. And awe leads us toward beauty. But it never will, if we do not nurture and sustain our initial surprise, wonder, and amazement of the new, different, and unexpected.

I call this practice "Cultivating Awe" because we are attempting to nurture a sustainable response to the unexpected that does not demand an automatic judgment or categorization. Awe, we remember, implies reverence and respect of the other and its otherness. We may not choose the other for ourselves, but it exists in the vast world and *all* its diverse aspects.

To Practice Being "Awe-ful"

1. Identify some small thing that habitually "puts you off." Try seeing/sensing it anew, as if for the first time. Can you move *back* to being amazed by it, as we are defining amazement here? How long can you stay there, in that amazed place, instead of launching into judgment? I've tried this with licorice. I really dislike black licorice. So I went and bought some, set it on the table in front of me, and tried to encounter it as if for the first time. I smelled it. I licked it. I finally nibbled on one end of the hard black square. Not one of my senses was attracted to that licorice; visually, I found it uninspiring, its smell

was unappealing, and its taste made my tongue cringe. My all-around response was repulsion. But, yes, I was amazed that I could be so repulsed by something that others clearly found pleasant and even an appealing treat! I wondered why I felt as I did. I was in awe that there were such strong preferences in us humans.

2. Now try cultivating your own awe around something of more significance for you. Is there a whiff of bigotry about you? Racism, sexism? Do you have a visceral reaction to a particular political dogma? Can you find amazement, some reverence, and respect for such otherness? Is it possible not to make it wrong, just different from your preferences? Play with this. For this practice, journaling can be very helpful. Get your thoughts down. Question yourself. Why does this "other" feel other to you?

3. Now, where does the wonder in your life tend to pop in? For me this often occurs while observing the natural world—watching the ocean, sky, bird busyness. Spend some time with and in wonder. Become familiar with how wonder feels. How, when does it enlarge into awe?

4. Find an old tree. Really perceive it. Think of all the years it has been rooted in that spot. What might it have experienced, witnessed? Imagine its sap pulsing through its veins like our own blood courses through our veins. You are two entities encountering one another. Can you feel awe?

5. Notice how this practice builds upon the previous one, "Practice Seeing."

Cultivating awe of the world and its organic, pulsating, often untidy unfurling is a challenging and always entertaining practice. It is all in allowing the attitude of being amazed to *stick*, not evaporate or morph into annoyance when the proverbial stuff hits the fan, as it often will, given there are so many energetic entities out there with intentions that may be counter to our own.

Really, think about that for a moment. We all go charging off into our days with our agendas in place, our intentions set. Others have *their* plans, intentions, and directions. Whether it is with partners or strangers, we may well butt heads against one another. A friend once defined a problem as two separate intentions colliding. Exactly!

Watching the attitudes with which we hold ourselves and present our behaviors and thoughts, consciously choosing them, will help bring inner peace, inner harmony. Inner beauty. We must be responsible for ourselves and our own states of being before we can positively contribute to another's, let alone take any degree of responsibility for any others'. Common sense, right? And I repeat, as within, so without.

III. Practice Operating in the Both/And Universe

The attempt to live according to the notion that the fragments are really separate is, in essence, what has led to the growing series of extremely urgent crises that is confronting us today.

—David Bohm

This practice is in response to the "either/or" mentality that governs so much of our thinking and reasoning these days. It is one of the major constructs in our automatic pilot reflex.

Dumping divisive duality does not mean we will all be the same. How boring would that be? Diversity, a much misused word and concept these days, is very different from duality. Noticing and enjoying differences (as in the Practice of Seeing) is very important. Pitting one difference against another, looking for better and worse values for petty reasons to divide and conquer, is what an ingrained either/or attitude may lead to, when used beyond the parameters of rational usefulness.

Holding a both/and attitude endeavors to see all sides before choice, if choice needs to made, is not always easy. But note, seeing is not the same as choosing for oneself. It does facilitate understanding. It puts that action of making a choice into a greater context, a more conscious context. And I believe that makes it a more beautiful action, one that contributes to a greater overall harmony.

A Story

Imagine a two-story, neutral-colored ball. It is huge. A strong light source is to one side, illuminating that side very brightly. Two people stand on either side of the ball. Each is asked what color the ball is. The person standing on the lit side states her truth: "this giant ball is bright white!"

The person standing on the other side of the ball states his truth: "This ball is black!" Consider this: Is either wrong? Are they both right?

If neither person moves from his or her position, the pair will argue forever, quite certain of the veracity of their perceptions. It is only after each is willing to walk around the sphere that they understand: they were both telling the truth, *their* truth, about that giant ball from their perspective.

That giant ball appeared *both* black *and* white. It wasn't *either* black *or* white…as is so very often the case in most of life.

Both/And Couples

I have several sets of couple friends who married despite their different religious beliefs and practices. In each case, their both/and approach to being together and raising a family made their lives possible. One couple was a Jewish/Mormon marriage, another Catholic/Jewish. A third was an atheist/Protestant partnership. Each family practiced all holidays and traditions that were significant to the family member individually, overlapping when necessary and celebrating the differences. Education and discussion were key. In one instance, I recall going to my friends' Passover Seder, and their children later joined in the neighborhood Easter egg hunt.

When I queried my Mormon friend how she thought her children were doing with their double-message religious education, she said, "They will make up their own minds as they grow up. At least they know about our values and ethics. God is God, my husband says, whatever flavor."

If any one of these people had held an either/or attitude, that person probably would not be with his or her current partner. "My religion or the door" would have kicked in at some point (hopefully before wedding bells and babies!).

By the way, I want to make it very clear that this does not mean I think one sort of marriage is more correct than another. No. I do not. But holding a both/and attitude opens up options and gives one the chance to consider all choices. One of those choices is to marry within your faith/culture/race. Or not.

The Importance of the Practice

We don't have to live in a polarizing, permanent, or fixed either/or paradigm. All around us is evidence of a both/and reality to remind us that we exist in a diverse, wondrous, amazingly inclusive, and paradoxically complex universe. Think of sweet *and* sour, acid *and* alkaline, black *and* white. The natural world did not choose between mammals or reptiles. It allowed for both hot- and cold-blooded creatures. Go figure!

The practice of True Beauty can act as an antidote to duality that becomes divisive.

Chaos theory, at least as presented by Briggs and Peat, contains a great deal of support for several of the beauty practices: humor, simplicity, and the both/and view, to name a few. Regarding a both/and practice, Briggs and Peat contributed insight to this saying:

> "One of our most persistent sources of confusion arises from our insistence on parceling the world into dualities. Expecting things to be either simple or complex is one example. Chaos theory points us beyond simplicity and complexity...[it] shows us that it is an illusion to separate the self from the other... the more energy we put into one pole of a duality, the more it takes the charge of its opposite. So what are we to do?...Chaos suggests that irony, metaphor, and humor help to move us beyond duality into a new clarity of vision."

As stated earlier, the either/or sorting method can have its usefulness. I am very much an advocate of making clear choices for ourselves. This is not about undermining that. What practicing living in the both/and universe is about is refining our process to reach those choices. A both/and personal universe is richer, deeper, and more inclusive.

The sharp knife of an either/or situation is still in the proverbial toolbox; it simply should not be used as unconsciously or as rapidly as we sometimes do. We all must make choices about some things at certain points; to make significant choices holding the both/and attitude is to make more conscious choices, more likely to be in greater harmony with your personal universe. Holding a both/and attitude makes one more aware of the field of infinite possibilities.

To Practice Living in the Both/And Universe

1. Notice each time you make a choice between one event/thing and another primarily because you feel one precludes the other. To notice is the beginning of awareness, of creating change when change is desired. In this case, such change might be discovering more possibility, the ability to create more inclusiveness.

2. Try some creative problem solving to open up some energy channels of possibility. I know too often I get fixated on something happening in a particular day/time/way, when truly there are other avenues.

   One of my favorite examples is a young couple I know who run their own labor-intensive business and have three children, a dog, and a cat. They were feeling they had little time for each other...until they realized that they could take off the occasional weekday afternoon with each other. The kids were in school, the work crews were out, and the part-time office help was on the phones. *Voila!* They had both private time together while having temporarily delegated all their other responsibilities.

   Remember that giant ball? See where else you can apply this idea. Where else can you look on the other side and see a problem from another vantage point or see another's truth? How does your pet view dinnertime? How do you? If you have a boss, how does she view her working conditions? How did the *other* political party come to their beliefs? Their solutions? Have fun with this.

3. When able, try dismissing time. Don't be as ruled by the clock as we all tend to be. Go forward without looking at clocks, and listen to your body's needs/ clock instead. You might find more time to include more—adding some "ands" into your life! But remember, an "and" might just be quiet time or time with your significant other.

4. When you start to disagree with someone, see if you can allow that viewpoint to coexist with your own—allowing both to be. *You needn't to agree; just let it be.*

5. Challenge yourself. Where have you, through habit more than choice, excluded something—an idea, a doingness, or someone—because you believed that it was an either/or circumstance. Is it truly?

Because True Beauty is about the reaching for harmony, this practice is essential to The Way of Beauty.

I find the best way to love someone
is not to change them,
but instead, help them reveal the greatest version of themselves.

—Steve Maraboli

IV. Practice Feeling Compassion

A human being is a part of the whole called by us universe, a part limited in time and space. He experiences himself, his thoughts and feeling as something separated from the rest, a kind of optical delusion of his consciousness. This delusion is a kind of prison for us, restricting us to our personal desires and to affection for a few persons nearest to us. Our task must be to free ourselves from this prison by widening our circle of compassion to embrace all living creatures and the whole of nature in its beauty.

—Albert Einstein

What is meant by "compassion"? It is an oft-used word in religious and spiritual spheres, but what does it really mean?

The word itself comes from the Latin *compati*, meaning "suffer with." Is it simply another word for empathy? My favorite dictionary, the multivolume *Oxford English Dictionary*, defines compassion as "sympathetic pity and concern for the sufferings or misfortunes of others." Frankly, I think this doesn't go far enough. It is an oversimplification for a word that is meant to represent a complex and deep state of not only a particular state of awareness, but being.

For our purposes, we will view sympathy, empathy, and compassion as gradients of the same root human inclination to feel for another, with sympathy being the "weak tea," a bit distant

Field is the only reality, there is no physical matter, only denser and denser fields.

—Albert Einstein

and uninvolved, empathy a stronger tea with deeper interest, and compassion...well, read on. Compassion is a foundational block of practicing True Beauty.

First, it is important to distinguish compassion from empathy, which is defined as "feeling *with* an other" and does not carry the same particular connotation and emphasis of suffering. Compassion is an important element in one's ability to become more spiritually aware and have greater consciousness. Empathy is a feeling that is primarily a product of the intellect, while compassion is specifically about the ability and willingness to know another's experience of pain. Most distinctively, compassion is a sensation, and it is a *field.*

Intriguing Invisible Fields

A field is a nonmaterial area of influence surrounding a material region, an energetic entity. Many scientists now posit that fields are more fundamental than any bit of matter (think atoms, subatomic particles). Fields are energies swirling together and, often, dancing with one another. Sometimes such fields actually allow energy to manifest as matter. While not a scientist, I will attempt to clarify and explain why fields are so integral to not only compassion but all the work and practices being done around evolving consciousness and spirituality.

We are learning more and more about the nature and importance of electromagnetic fields (EMF) every day. The World Health Organization says natural sources of "electromagnetic fields are present everywhere in our environment but are invisible to the human eye. Electric fields are produced by the local build-up of electric charges in the atmosphere... The earth's magnetic field causes a compass needle to orient in a North-South direction and is used by birds and fish for navigation."

The human body's nervous system is its electrical system. We are electrical "objects." Each organ in the body, as well as the body as a whole, emits its own EMF. There are several ways in which this informs our world, but for right now, all we need to understand is that such fields carry information back and forth. Sometimes the brain is the last to know.

And there is another sort of field: the morphogenic field. Rupert Sheldrake's research evolved this once genetics-related hypothesis and expanded on it to include the concept of "morphic resonance." About this he said the following:

> Morphic resonance thus involves the influence of like upon like, the influence of patterns of activity on subsequent similar patterns of activity, an influence that passes through or across space and time from past to present. These influences do not to fall off with distance in space or time. The greater the degree of similarity of the systems involved, the greater the influence of morphic resonance.
>
> Morphic resonance gives an inherent memory in fields at all levels of complexity. In the case of squirrels, each individual squirrel draws upon, and in turn contributes to, a collective or pooled memory of its kind. In the human realm, this kind of collective memory corresponds to what the psychologist C. G. Jung called the collective unconscious…Morphic resonance should be detectable in the realms of physics, chemistry, biology, animal behavior, psychology and the social sciences.

Not to get confused here, but please remember I am talking about compassion—the *sensation* of compassion. In her definitive book *Field of Compassion,* Judy Cannato states that "a new morphogenic field characterized by compassion is emerging." Remember that I said empathy is an intellectual endeavor, but compassion is more than that—an actual experience? It takes a story to explain this best, and I will use one from Sheldrake's own work, *Psychological Perspectives,* (1987).

A Story

In England in the 1920s, it was usual to deliver fresh milk every morning to each home's doorstep. The bluetit, a common bird of the region, was seen pecking open the cardboard milk caps and drinking the cream off the top. Some reports declared that the birds would even follow the milkman down the street as he made his deliveries. The first recorded incident of the cream-sipping bluetits was in 1921. According to birdwatchers of the time, the habit continued to spread hundreds of miles away, which was surprising as the bluetits rarely flew farther than a fifteen-mile radius from their nests.

Evidently, by 1947, the cute, if annoying, little habit had spread remarkably—milk bottle tops were being opened by bluetits all over England, Sweden, Holland, and Denmark. But around 1939–1940, milk delivery in Holland was halted due to the German occupation; the birds had no access to their milk! Doorstep delivery did not start again until eight years later in 1948, about five years longer than the average life-span of the bluetit. Yet within months after the reappearance of milk on the doorsteps, the birds were back at it!

How had this happened? How had these later generations "learned" of this food source? For that matter, how had it spread so far to begin with? Behaviors inherited directly from past members of a species – morphic resonance.

The Importance of the Practice

Those little birds carried the knowing as gnowing. It was what we might (if we didn't know better) call instinctual. But how did that new instinct come into being? How to get at that cream! How to know that there even *was* cream in those weird things on doorsteps!

Cannato theorizes that compassion itself is an experiential exchange between beings, in fact a field that is naturally shared, literally without thinking. Sheldrake appears to agree when he says that what we learn is not held in our brains, but in morphogenic fields, through morphic resonances. The bringing to consciousness of this learning is acknowledging our own gnowing.

To transcend from mere intellect or feeling to the broader experiential sensation that is compassion involves the employment of our fields of energies, to actually engage with and feel another's suffering to a degree without having gone through the causal pain. Imagine fields of information passing back and forth—and our heart's willingness to accept compassion's field of information knock, knocking on its door.

When asked, "In your opinion, what differentiates empathy from compassion?" a friend of mine (who happens to be a Sister of Mercy) thought for a moment and then said, "Compassion comes from the heart. The heart. It is much deeper than empathy."

At first, I was disappointed in her answer. Humph! The heart! Then I remembered some of my own research and indeed one of these Beauty Practices—Think with the Heart—and I realized, "Of course! Compassion originates from and within the heart *field*!" Or rather, when we "*think*" with the heart, we have a realization *and sensation* in the heart's field: experiencing compassion for another. It is not only a thought, a feeling; it is an experience that often prompts activity. More about EMFs and their significance in walking the Way of Beauty crop up later in these pages, one of them being the practice on how to think with your heart.

By the way, this True Beauty activity is purposely not expressed as "practice *being* compassionate" as I don't know if one can *be* compassionate until one has really learned to feel compassion on a regular basis. If compassion doesn't come naturally—and it may not with all people—then one must "exercise the muscle" to best use it with ease and regularity.

Compassion is the root expression of our awareness of the *universality* of the ability to experience pain, no matter its origin or reason, no matter the species, race, intelligence, or preferences. We have *all* experienced some sort of pain. That simple fact is the unifying factor underlying the ability to practice compassion and distinguish it from mere empathy.

Compassion is the great leveler, the great unifying knowing. The Dalai Lama has been widely quoted as saying, "If you want others to be happy, practice compassion. If you want to be happy, practice compassion."

Suppressing compassion causes harmful complications. If we can objectify an Other, disassociate ourselves from "Them," it is easy to find fault, *un*-beauty. Once, however, we can *experience* compassion, we can practice *being compassionate* from a place of sincerity without artifice.

And compassion is said to be the basis of all morality.

Currently, science is positing that compassion may not come naturally to everyone. Evidently, some are unable or choose not to see pain in others.

In brain-imaging tests, evidence of specifically different emotional stimuli were revealed as emanating from particular areas in the brain. Men and women were tested to show and compare areas of such brain activity. The tests revealed that some men exhibited little or *no activity* in the area of the brain where compassion was usually seen to be expressed.

Does this mean the male of our species isn't capable of compassion? Of course not. But it may mean that there is not as natural and easy a predisposition to recognizing and experiencing compassion in the male brain, for whatever reasons. A quick overview of our world history of aggression while under patriarchal domination does tend to support this hypothesis.

But evidently, compassion can be taught! Yay! Hence, the practice of *feeling* compassion—exercise the muscle. Follow the Way of Beauty and become more compassionate.

To Practice Feeling Compassion

1. Stop watching any entertainment media (television, movies, etc.) that regularly or primarily depict another's pain and suffering. While these are just stories and dramatizations, and because you are a removed observer only, you are teaching yourself to resist compassion, to see suffering and *not feel.* At best you will feel fear, terror, disgust—and know it to be false, undeserved. You can turn it off with a flip of a switch and attention. Sound silly? It isn't.

   These days, we are so inundated with images of suffering, violence, and degradation of others. It is an unbidden assault on our psyches, and we are tempted to become thick skinned, jaded, and unfeeling. It is almost impossible not to, especially when we start our viewing as children. We learn early to defend our psyches from becoming overwhelmed with gratuitous depictions of suffering on TV and in movies and thus fall into the danger of becoming inured to the suffering of others. What we are watching is just a story, and since we are being a removed observer of what on one level we know is fictional, we teach ourselves that to react to the stimuli coming at us is unnecessary. We bar feelings that might be uncomfortable, like compassion. The psychic scab becomes too thick, eventually, to even feel real-life compassion, common compassion—for the scenes of war on that screen, or the pain of a pet, of our brother, sister, or neighbor.

So do an experiment. For two weeks, turn off your TV. If that is not possible, watch only those films that have no war, murder, rape, or apocalypse-type fear-mongering in them, and do not watch any news. After the two weeks, check in with yourself: Are you sleeping better? Are you less anxious? Feeling more productive, creative? Having more conversations with others? Consider going for another week. And if or when you do choose to tune back in ration the amount of "storied suffering" you imbibe. There is enough in the real world.

2. To exercise your compassion muscle, try feeling like some other species. This is a variation on the "walk a mile in another's shoes" lesson. It's fun and easy. Sit outside and *be* that butterfly flitting about. Have a cat or a dog? Get down on the floor and look at the world from its perspective, literally. This is the beginning of playing with being able to feel another's experience.

3. Facilitate your "field work!" Being aware of our own EMFs and the existence of our ability to resonate (or not) with our environments and other beings around us is a tremendous advantage. This awareness allows us to tap into and perhaps more directly control and empower what is happening in our fields.

   Imagination is a wonderful thing. Our ability to visualize something we haven't actually seen (my heart's field? A quark?) will help it to materialize. I am not making this up. It has been proven in the physics lab. And I believe an essential foundation block for feeling compassion is our ability to imagine the other. In so doing, are we in fact opening up our field to theirs. We are increasing the incidence of morphic resonance.

So try it. Some of the ways to do this might sound creepy, at first—but they are not creepy when done with empathy, in search of compassion. For instance, imagine looking through another person's eyes. What does that person see from his or her vantage point? Where was that person before he or she was with you? What might that person be juggling in his or her brain? Now, what is he or she feeling this very moment? Can you ask? Is a belt too tight, cutting into his or her waist, distracting subtly from the discussion? Feel that tightness. Is there a foot or finger tap-tapping? Try it. What is it telling you about the other person?

4. Conversely...don't forget to have compassion for yourself, as well. This is something I still have to work at. My goal one year was this: "Be kind to yourself, Lisa!" What does this mean? Too often, we are our own harshest critics. Got only a B+ on that exam? Shame! Just because you had surgery last month and have been doing physical therapy three times a week is no excuse for being behind on your month's sales quota! Get with it! How 'bout, "Isn't that baby fat gone *yet?* The baby came home two weeks ago!"

   You get the picture...our expectations of ourselves too often hold little compassion, no allowance for any suffering or pain, for transitional needs, for any margin of error. We can hold our suffering at bay, not allowing it in, feeling it, and allowing it to be real, true.

   We might spin off here into the illusions of perfectionism, but that is for later.

Now we are addressing being compassionate toward ourselves, understanding, and forgiving of ourselves as we go forward doing the best that we can with the information and the tools at hand under the circumstances we have created for ourselves—with the understanding that nothing is static. Life and we are evolving. Recognize your suffering, but don't let it rule you—either by assiduously ignoring it or by placing it on the throne and becoming its servant. And perhaps most importantly, endeavor not to disassociate from your pain. It is not an *other.* It is part of you. There is no "it" and "me."

As stated earlier, compassion is the basis of all morality and, I posit, the basis and central portal into the awareness of True Beauty.

True Beauty is the ever-evolving harmonies that occur in our everyday experiences, perceptions, and indeed in our cosmos. Compassion is the perception, the key ingredient that neutralizes the sense of "otherness" that distances us from each other. We are all particular units of the One. Compassion must be in the toolbox of all who are interested in helping along the paradigm shift from conflict-centric to cooperative-centric.

V. Think with Your Heart

Intuition is the clear conception of the whole at once.

—Johann Kaspar Lavater

How often have we heard in popular culture, "It broke my heart!" or "That went straight to my heart." Or how about, "I hold him/her/it close to my heart."

What do we mean when we say, feel, and think these things? What are we actually acknowledging? Most of us, when pressed, will dismiss these phrases, thinking, "Oh, that's just a saying!" Yet we actually *do* perceive and think using our hearts. These sayings exist because we gnow this and use that gnowingness frequently, some might say as second nature.

There is, in fact, quite a bit of science to support the existence of the heart's ways of knowing and understanding. An extremely interesting organization, the HeartMath Institute, has delved into the subject. "The heart is the most powerful generator of electromagnetic energy in the human body...The heart's electrical field is about 60 times greater in amplitude than the electrical activity generated by the brain...Furthermore, the magnetic field produced by the heart is more than 5,000 times greater in strength than the field generated by the brain, and can be detected a number of feet away from the body, in all directions." (*Head-Heart Interactions*, www.heartmath.org/research/science-of-the-heart/soh_20.html.2007.)

Further, the neural network that most of us were educated to believe was the purview of the brain alone is—surprise!—a web throughout our entire body. In fact, some are making a distinction between the brain and the "heartbrain."

What does that imply? This: we "think" from all over. Our current culture has habitually discounted the heart's information-gathering ability and, in turn, how it informs us. The HeartMath Institute data, among others, suggest that sometimes the heart bypasses the brain, but oftentimes it works *with* the brain. If it is the heart alone passing information, we may name that knowing as intuition. When our brain and heart are working together in coherence, we might experience that as our inner voice. The data further suggest that when the heart and the brain are working together coherently, we make our best choices, have the clearest thoughts, and optimize our creativity.

Ever hear of a maker, artist, or athlete talk about being in the flow? It is that zone in which everything is happily coming together, going well, and time just flies by. I think that is when we are primarily thinking and acting with our hearts, and our brains and bodies are in concert. We are one lovely symphony producing what it is we are moved to do.

Yahoo!

The Importance of the Practice

The age of reason and logic presided over by the almighty brain needs to be over. Reason and logic have their places; it is just not on the throne (as we remember from the Both/And Practice). They are tools of the thought process but limited ones when isolated and considered alone. I am in no way discounting their benefits.

Great for measurement and calculation, the age of reason and logic, unaccompanied by inspiration, intuition, and aesthetics, devolved into a hollow, simplistic, and spiritually devoid era.

I should make something clear here. When I refer to the age of reason and logic, I am taking a bit of poetic license in that I am not referring to Thomas Paine's definition of the Age of Reason. That was, in fact, an altogether other philosophy and thought thread that was quite useful in liberating the minds of nineteenth-century humankind and challenging the hold of the Christian church. Rather, I mean to give a title to what we have seen growing since the early twentieth century: the idea that if something cannot be scientifically proven by modern scientific methods (read: seen/felt/touched, measured, weighed, quantified), it cannot be real.

While uncovering and measuring some interesting physical stuff and contributing greatly to our knowledge base, this path of scientific-centric thinking also led us down some very constricted and dark alleys. It dismissed the invisible; it somehow cast faith in the unseen into the abyss of charlatans.

The dark alley most pervasive in our culture—and very damaging to the spiritually inclined—is that "show me!" meme. It has been so hammered into the generations since the Industrial Revolution that the majority of people in Western culture now believe it is only sensible to think that if we cannot see/feel/hear it, it cannot be real.

Ironically enough, science is now proving in its reductionistic, Cartesian way how wrongheaded it has been. And I love the paradox! It is, actually, a thing of True Beauty! (OK, I must direct your attention to a few of the Beauty Practices that this turn of events illustrates: Both/And Universe, Be Wary of the Truth, and—of course—Seeing. Read on!)

Observation not only disturbs what has to be measured, they produce it. We compel the electron to assume a definite position. We ourselves produce the results of the measurement.

-http://media.noetic.org/uploads/files/PhysicsEssays-Radin-DoubleSlit-2012.pdf

Through its obsessive, matter-oriented, mechanistic navel gazing, the quantum physics-oriented crowd is discovering that the long-held gap and dichotomy between science and faith is rapidly disappearing—faith being the word to express belief in that which cannot be readily or easily seen, measured, or quantified. In other words, not scientifically provable.

So imagine the surprise of some of those scientists when they only found what they were looking for when they were able to imagine it!

The quantum double-slit experiment is a great example of how consciousness and our physical material world are intertwined. One potential revelation of this experience is that "the observer creates the reality." Published in the peer-reviewed journal *Physics Essays*, a paper explains how this experiment has been used multiple times to explore the role of consciousness in shaping the nature of physical reality.

The folk wisdom of many cultures has known much of this—the Dine of North America, the Tuvans of what is now the Republic of Tuva in Russia, as well as the Mayan and Aztec cultures. It is known/gnown that we create our own realities, often referring to the heart as a center of knowing, wisdom, and feeling, that we are one: spirit, matter, and mind. Now our god of science has validated that knowingness—or more correctly, gnowingness—beginning with the astounding data that the heart has a greater electromagnetic field than the brain. It has an abundance of neural networks. We do, in fact, think with our hearts. We know. We have always gnown, though we may have become temporarily blind to what we were actually doing.

Now our best minds are beginning to sense and study our gnowingness (though they don't use this word for it—yet). At

A fundamental conclusion of the new physics also acknowledges that the observer creates the reality. As observers, we are personally involved with the creation of our own reality. Physicists are being forced to admit that the universe is a "mental" construction. Pioneering physicist Sir James Jeans wrote: "The stream of knowledge is heading toward a non-mechanical reality; the universe begins to look more like a great thought than like a great machine. Mind no longer appears to be an accidental intruder into the realm of matter, we ought rather hail it as the creator and governor of the realm of matter. Get over it, and accept the inarguable conclusion. The universe is immaterial-mental and spiritual."

–R. C. Henry, "The Mental Universe," *Nature*

the Institute of HeartMath, researchers also conducted a study on intuition. Their findings showed "strong evidence for the proposition that intuitive processes involve the body accessing a field of information that is not limited by the constraints of space and time."

Whether one can buy into this wholeheartedly or not, such data, along with other research, certainly helps me take more seriously that "little voice" inside my head when I am confronted with a decision.

To Practice Thinking with Your Heart

1. Do not dismiss those thoughts and impulses you've previously labeled as intuition when they arise. They *are* intuition, and they are a way of knowing and receiving information. Take the action, speak them out loud, or write them down.

2. Listen for and to your inner voice(s). (I have a few, and no, I don't have multiple personalities.) What are you feeling? If it is a surge of love or loving kindness, express it! Walk across that crowded meeting room to pay the compliment that just drifted into your head.

3. Experiment with "body knowing." Listen to what your body is telling you it wants for fuel in the moment. Licorice? Go for it! To me, listening to my body means to kind of scan my body. Am I wanting food? What sort? Does my body want exercise? Rest? What body part aches? Is it a good

ache from exercise or a complaining ache from misuse? Be kind and responsive to your body. Heartfelt.

Sometimes I imagine all the zillions of cells that make up all the plasma, veins, muscles, and organs in there. They all have jobs to do. We are taught that they are "autonomic systems"—that they have their instructions and are performing them automatically. That word again. Well, while that is probably part of the truth, I also talk to my cells, saying, "Thanks for doing your job!"—when they are. Because I have major systems that are *not* doing their jobs as they are supposed to (e.g., epilepsy), I ask, "What can I do from out here to help?" Meaning, is there any action I can initiate using my heart-directed conscious mind that will help that system overcome the inherent challenges being faced.

The body is one very complex, interconnected vehicle that houses us—mind and soul—and we can communicate with all departments, not just those that feel or seem to be controlled by the brain in our head.

4. Choose to be around higher companions. I bet you know what I mean—those people who help you laugh, lighten your spirit, and emanate enthusiasm. These are the friends who lend intelligent encouragement and critical analysis when needed. You've heard yourself think or say about them, "I just *love* spending time with (insert name here)." We associate "love" with our hearts, yes?

   It is time to stop ignoring what we come to know and feel in a manner we think of as "intuitively." If something is calling to us, moving us, or inspiring us that has no logical source or outcome—so what? Get over it!

> Practice thinking with your heart. Allow yourself. It is beautiful. Full of beauty. And the results may be surprising, in a good way.

Thinking with your heart supports and nourishes True Beauty in a few ways. Most basically, it hones the vessel that is you, making you clearer and more tuned in to a primary way of gnowing. It contributes greatly to one's ability to be true to oneself, authentic. Heart thinking helps you steer clear of those who may drag you down. At the very least, it will help make you aware of that dynamic and therefore be in greater control around your interactions with those people and circumstances. You will be kinder to yourself and to others, I'll betcha!

The intuitive mind is a sacred gift and the rational mind is a faithful servant. We have created a society that honors the servant and has forgotten the gift.

—Albert Einstein

VI. Practice Being Wary of "Truth"

The great enemy of the truth is very often not the lie—deliberate, contrived, and dishonest—but the myth—persistent, persuasive, and unrealistic.

—President John F. Kennedy

Beware truth!

This is one of my favorite Beauty Practices, in part because it has a certain shock value for some people first hearing of it—and I can be mischievous. But mostly because it is a constant practice for me. It is a constant challenge to my daily- operating assumptions.

During my master's studies, I heard about how scientists today hold and work with the concept of theory. Even though I have been a patient all my life, I hadn't really thought about terms like *accepted medical theory* or *current science.* It turns out there can be a particularly skeptical attitude toward scientific theory. Why? Because a theory is just a *best guess* based on some evidence. Among some researchers, there is even an initialism for it: SAFN or *s*omewhat *a*dequate *f*or *n*ow.

For example, inquiry into a realm of the largely unknown (say, dark energy or neuroscience) would continue until an apparent pattern or story began to form from the clues and evidence that was accrued. That story was then extrapolated into a probable scenario and, with a certain amount of agreement among the relevant parties involved, deemed a bona fide theory.

The dictionary definition of theory is "speculation, assumption, conjecture." So a theory left unchallenged by new or different speculation, assumption, or information starts to be considered a working theory or "truth" (SAFN) by scientists and researchers and as truth by the general public, who are merely following the scientists' suit. Often, it is the very longevity of a theory that seems to underwrite its status as proof of its veracity. Think the big bang theory or the theory of relativity. Once it was the theory that the sun revolved around the earth…or that the earth (clearly!) is flat!

You get the idea. Not too long ago, we thought the atom was the smallest particle in the universe. We now know that is not the case. In fact (funny choice of wording in this section, eh?), we now know we have yet to know what the smallest particle might be and are, at this writing, still searching for it. (In my next life, I may have to be a theoretical physicist—it is such a mysterious frontier!)

What I am endeavoring to say here is that like so many other things, truth is not static. It changes, evolves. A truth will work and be useful for a period of time and then may morph in response to the factors surrounding it, some of which will be humankind's ability to know and understand the depth and scope of those factors. This is why we must be "wary of the truth" to practice True Beauty. To be mired in fixed ideas is the antithesis of being aware of and open to True Beauty. It is like having blinders on. And most importantly, too often an assumption of truth can function as validation for our automatic pilot.

No such thing as a solid, eternal truth? OMG! Does that make you nervous, a little anxious, maybe? Well, you can relax.

Truth as we commonly understand it is still a useful and vital concept. The "shared truth" of a society helps to create a generally accepted sense of what is predictable and can be expected—in short, what is "real." This in turn shapes and integrates core cultural ethics and intention that in its turn sets the expectations for and helps create a more harmonious society. And this is precisely the goal of practicing True Beauty—harmony. That it is continually evolving makes it no less powerful. We must simply acknowledge this evolution and—most importantly—evolve along with it.

Again, this is why the way of True Beauty and its practice was born. I believe that it is critical *now* that we remain conscious of not just our evolving cultures and planet, but of our evolving cosmos, and that through increased awareness and practice of True Beauty, we each, so simply and delightfully, improve our abilities to contribute to smooth evolutions toward greater harmonies. As individuals, we are absolutely able to make a difference. It is the butterfly effect in each of our hands.

As Brian Swimme, professor and cosmologist, has said, "The universe is expanding exactly as it must"—including all the dogmas, doctrines, and "truths" that have gone before, exist today, and are currently in vogue, and those truths that are still awaiting discovery.

A Story

We have only to look at history to see how what is perceived as true evolves. There are even historical events illustrating how evolving truth has affected our application and attitudes around beauty. In fact, I wonder if the following series of events was not the final nails in the coffin of True Beauty in modern times.

Aestheticism incorporated the belief that beauty was above concepts such as right and wrong (those moral and didactic issues), and yet in the end, it seems to me to have evolved its own brand of elitist hierarchy.

Aestheticism was art centric. Based on the philosopher Emmanuel Kant, following the French *l'art pour l'art,* aestheticism beauty became too synonymous with art. Beauty is not confined to or articulated by art alone, as we will examine later. Further, in aestheticism, there appears an inference that nature itself is rather mundane, needing improvement through man's orchestration and creation of art.

One of this movement's most prominent spokesmen was Oscar Wilde. Born in 1854, Wilde lectured often and vociferously on the importance of art and beauty in people's everyday lives. He is quoted as saying "We spend our days looking for the secret of life. Well, the secret of life is art." He also said, "Even a color-sense is more important in the development of the individual than a sense of right and wrong."

Aestheticism emerged in response, in part, to the influences of utilitarianism and the then newly flourishing Industrial Revolution and the mechanization of many previously hand-wrought items. Along the way, the aestheticism movement seems to have become burdened with an arrogant attitude of "know best" that alienated its adherents from the majority of the population—that is, the group that would come to be classified as the working class. An artist, a creator of beauty, was considered superior—a duality newly minted out of industrialization, I think. All of those who had previously been artisans—makers of furniture, metal work, woodwork, and so on, many of whom were now manning the factories—were no longer considered to have enough taste to appreciate the arts as conceived by aestheticism's aesthetes. While lauding "art for art's sake," aestheticism's adherents did not appear capable of recognizing the ubiquitous nature of beauty or the wide diversity of its makers.

All in all, aestheticism seems to have devolved into an excellent example of blinkered arrogance, a negative form of elitism raising its nasty head in relation to the promulgation of the concept of beauty. It started with a noble intent, yet refused the broader and spiritual component that could provide the context for its far-reaching constructs and the implications for all of humankind.

Aestheticism had the idea correct—beauty is important—but the scope and execution wrong. It's not just about "art," or the sculpting—supposed improvement—of the wild by a few. It is not only about refuting the current cultural trends in morality. It is not just *l'artiste* who can sense beauty or create it. The sheer universality of beauty's truth appears to have been missed by Wilde and his cohorts. But their initial impulse was on track. Now we must make some corrections and move forward.

There is an axiom in organizational development circles: "Just because an idea (or product, or process) didn't work in the past, doesn't mean it won't work *now*. Review and reevaluate."

Or, one might ask, "Is it still true?"

Beauty and its integral-yet-transcendent nature is an idea whose time has always been. I am bold enough to say that True Beauty is the litmus paper we may use to check *any* supposed truth. Now, hopefully, we are mature enough as beings, able enough, conscious enough, to review, reevaluate, and go forward anew. Now is the time to recognize the inherent nature and *eternal* importance of True Beauty for the human condition and our planet's well-being.

The Importance of the Practice

As must be clear by now, I don't really believe in truth as I understand adherents of science and the age of reason to use and define it. Apparent from the above, I find truth to be relative, subjective. This can shock my more fundamentalist friends—whether they be vegan, Christian, pagan, or Democrat. And I have been delighted to discover that many quantum physicists, unlike their reductionistic predecessors, would agree.

It validates the Way of True Beauty hypothesis as well to find that the father of process philosophy, Alfred North Whitehead, places truth in a secondary position to beauty. He states unequivocally, "Beauty is a wider, and more fundamental notion than Truth." And then he goes on to say, "Truth matters because of Beauty." I encourage you to think about that.

The practice of being wary of the truth is an important safeguard against getting stuck in one particular place about any particular topic or belief. It is not designed to undercut faith (which is not completely knowledge based or fact based, which is why it is deemed "faith"), but to help us keep an open mind in all things. I believe it can even facilitate faith.

J. Krishnamurti, an Indian philosopher, had this to say about the nature of truth: "Truth is not a fixed point; it is not static; it cannot be measured by words; it is not a concept, an idea to be achieved."

To Practice "Truth Wariness"

1. Integrate the fluidity of truth into your consciousness.

   OK, that sounds like a mouthful. But let's break it down:

   a. First, accept the fluidity of truth. You can play with this by thinking about something you hold as definite. Challenge yourself to question it: Is it really definite permanently, or is it a truth you hold *right now* that has the potential, power, and possibility to grow and change over time, evolve? Does your choice to hold onto this truth as a static entity impede growth in some areas of your life? Ah, perhaps there is room for a different-yet-valid version of truth? Or for your idea of it to evolve?

   b. Consider that a truth is a story that someone has latched onto. When it flies in the face of "our" story, then we have conflict. Be flexible in your perspective on truth. Become aware of possible historical shifts. Know that one person's truth may not be another's. And both may well be correct.

   c. And finally, reject anything touting itself as an absolute truth (including this statement).

2. Deeply listen to yourself.

   How does one go about this? And what does this have to do with truth? To answer the second question first, we must first try to tell ourselves our *own* truths. This is explored more later in the Practice of Authenticity. So, to listen to ourselves, tap into and explore those other ways of knowing—develop your gnowingness. Whether it is through sitting silently, an art activity, or intense athletic activity—you probably already gnow what is going to exercise your gnowing self. Too often we do not listen to ourselves—those inner voices, and there may be a few of them.

Do not dismiss your intuition. It is a powerful way of knowing through gnowing. All the information that is pouring into your electromagnetic field can be accessed if you stop to look and listen for it. Your thoughts and insights are not just the background music of your actions. The old "stop, look, and listen" that children are taught to do at street corners is actually a good direction for listening to yourself. Stop doing, start looking inward, and start listening to those messages in there. Some of those ideas in the back of your head may come forward, and you might be surprised at what they have to share with you:

- Perhaps you really *don't* want to go to that game with that group.
- You *are* ready to start that project, and that piece of driftwood you saw last week is the perfect way to start it.
- Since he said that, does it mean the house *is* going to be for sale?

It is amazing what comes down that inner street when we stop, look, and listen!

And to practice deeply listening to yourself is to keep tabs on your own truth as well as where it may be heading. One can avoid having fixed ideas about oneself! Yahoo!

3. Remember, express your own truth with compassion for others.

   This, of course, can be done successfully (as defined by True Beauty) only if we are able to be sensitive to the positions of others, if we are able to walk around that huge ball, aware of others' world views.

   We see too much arrogance already in today's world. Yes, arrogance. There is nothing more arrogant than someone who, believing a truth to be the *only* truth, tells it with no apparent concern or sensitivity for those he or she is telling it to. This is the dynamic behind virtually every religious war; each side believes God is on their side. It is what has seeped into and now taken over too much global politics. "My truth is correct, and therefore you are wrong, hence you are less, *inferior.*" This attitude is the very definition of narrow-minded, unable to see or have respect for another's position.

4. Craft evolutionary communications.

   Communicate your truth with the intent to create an *evolutionary* response, not only from those with whom you communicate, but within yourself as well. This goes back to that old right/wrong thing. One way a communication is not going to evolve an issue is when it is one that is endeavoring to make me "right" and him "wrong."

   An evolutionary statement or response is one that reflects both truths and a different truth that is evolving from the two opposing truths. By helping differing truths understand one another, the response is evolutionary. It may have shades of old truths mingled with the new; it may be a striking comparison or new coupling. And it is most important to remember: you do not have to agree with the other's viewpoint in order to understand it.

To best employ evolutionary statements and responses requires nothing new or different from what has already been laid out here. This skill is in the same wheelhouse as *all* the "Be Wary of the Truth" practices as well as the "Cultivate Awe" practices. That is, strive not to cultivate those pesky fixed ideas. Try to be amazed, even awed, at differences in ideas and behaviors!

In the privacy of your own head, or in conversation with friends, look at those things you have always believed to be so but never really questioned. *Nothing is static.* Allow change to flow through your life and experiences as it must. This is not to say that one cannot rush it or slow it down when and how you can—but know and gnow your limits. Employ patience, tolerance, and yes, faith when needed.

And you and your responses, like truth, will evolve.

Now all these come together and you are best able to:

5. Tell yourself the truth. I've always said, "If I am lying to myself, I am automatically lying to everyone else!" Maybe *lying* is too harsh a word. Often it is just misrepresentation from not checking back in to what is *really* my truth. Do your best to tell yourself your truth. It is the Way of True Beauty. And it will help to create harmony in the cosmos. Cool, huh?!

   Now that you are telling yourself the truth, as best as you are able (and trust me, I get that it is not easy!), try this next idea.

6. Make choices that move you in your desired direction.

   This is a variation on two old chestnuts: "Find your truth/dream/purpose and follow it" and "the journey begins with a single step." The point here is that every step, every choice, takes you in a direction. Is it a direction you *want* to go in? Or are you just wandering about?

   Is that step/choice/direction you are about to take in sync with your purpose? Have you articulated your intentions to yourself? Your purpose? And are your choices taking you in that direction or away from it? We hear a lot about mindfulness these days. This is just a prompt to help you be more mindful of your choice of actions, both big and small.

   Some steps, some choices are bigger than others and therefore more difficult to reverse or change. This applies as well to the direction of our thoughts. But all steps take us in some direction, no matter how big or small. So ask the question: is it your *desired direction*?

   Sometimes I feel a general anxiety that I am not able to pin on any one thing or event. I have learned that it means there is some step or direction I have taken that is leading me off my path. Some of these choices have been mammoth and taken years to correct. Others were more mundane and easily fixable (like playing video games in the morning instead of writing).

   Making choices that keep us on our chosen paths is a major part of keeping us in harmony with ourselves, and therefore in True Beauty.

Do you see how all these "Be Wary of the Truth Practices" work together? They are a cycle, really—one leading to the other and back again. There are myriad truths that are swimming and morphing out there in the world, and we interact with them all the time. Then there are our own evolving inner truths, which weave the fabric of our spirits, albeit usually more slowly. These practices keep our truths supple and shiny, so True Beauty may shine through.

VII. Practice Authenticity

If I am not for myself, who will be?
If I am only for myself, what am I?
If not now, when?
—Rabbi Hillel, *The Talmud*

Or should it be "*awe*-thenticity"? Just being humorous (another Beauty Practice, incidentally), something that is authentically, well, *me*. It would be an oxymoron to say there is a set way to practice authenticity. However, since it is *my* authentic self to virtually always have something to say about almost everything, I certainly have something to say about this topic.

We are all barometers of our own authenticity. Those pesky internal barometers reflect our inner weather changes on many levels: moods, energy, integrity (often heard as the voice of conscience). While we sometimes know when we aren't being ourselves, don't we always *gnow* when we aren't? Isn't there that niggling feeling inside, a sense of pushing aside one intention or thought and replacing it with another?

For me, that was more pronounced, more readily visible to me, as a child, before I taught myself to become so much better at ignoring that uncomfortable feeling. Peer pressure enters and can go a long way in perfecting the suppression of our authenticity. We are human, after all. We enjoy approval, validation from our peer group—whomever, whatever that group might be at the moment. We confuse these things with love.

The antithesis of personal authenticity is the culturally embedded "Now-I'm- Supposed-Tos," or NISTs, as I call them. You know what I'm talking about. NISTs are the currency of both peer pressure and societal pressure to be and achieve certain things in a certain order. Now- I'm- Supposed-To: go to college, get a job, get married, have children, just to name a few of the more universal NISTs prevalent in our culture.

Ridding ourselves of these NISTs is easier said than done. Yet to do so, to recognize your own NISTs and evaluate them in terms of your authentic self, is to move ever closer to achieving inner harmony. And for us complex and sometimes (oftentimes?) confused humans, achieving inner harmony creates our own inner beauty.

Here is the thing that you probably gnow, but I will state out loud, so to speak: inner harmony must be the greater portion before we can spread and achieve harmony and True Beauty without.

Listening to and being our authentic selves is not necessarily about getting what we want. It *is* about responding authentically to the environment and influences around us. It is not necessarily about the outcomes of our choices and actions; it *is* about the process of making those choices and taking an action in ways real and true for us. Therein lies authenticity.

The Importance of the Practice

Practicing to become more authentically oneself is important in The Way of Beauty because each of us has our own uniqueness; each of us is an artisan of our experience. This uniqueness is an integral factor in keeping the balance of the many within the one. Balance that produces harmony. Once we stray from our authentic selves, we start dabbling in inner discord. Remaining authentic is about sustaining inner harmony…and, of course, as within, so without.

Our authenticity is not a static state to identify and then rest in. What is true for our innermost self can shift over time. Plus, at every stage of life as we grow and change, it seems new NISTs can evolve as well. This can be wonderful when they align with our inner desires and abilities, but when they don't, it can be very difficult. "Life's challenges," we euphemistically call them. And sometimes our authentic self is not in sync with cultural norms. Then what?

This brings up an integral point. A very important aspect of being our authentic self is to recognize that none of us is perfect. That being authentic is not always, uh, lovely. While I believe most people are good at their core, many experience what religious speak deems "temptation," those thoughts and brain pictures of actions that are culturally and/or morally unacceptable, that may even shock us as they cross our mental screens. And then there are those behaviors we may have exhibited in our younger years, perhaps as teenagers, when we were trying out different lifestyles. What is our true self, what is only passing, and how do we act on those temptations/deviations if they pop into our heads? These are our questions here.

Again, while most people are inherently good, some are not. For some, to be authentic means to go against the grain of what is generally morally and legally accepted in our society. But I am not speaking merely of societal notions here. As Elaine Scarry points out in *Beauty and Being Just*, there is a direct connection between True Beauty and justice, and I leave this close examination in her excellent hands. My point is that we must each come to know and embrace our true selves, warts and all, and work at staying in alignment with ourselves. If that authentic self is essentially antisocial—there are decisions to be made, with work and work-arounds if one chooses to do them.

A Story

I once knew someone whose behavior baffled me for many years until I realized that her authentic self was in battle, every day, with both socially acceptable behavior and her own NISTs.

From the baby boomer generation and an urban upper-middle-class family, Gretchen's NISTs centered around certain liberal sociopolitical ideals of that time that, prompted by her mother, she had chosen to embrace: pacifism, women's rights, consciousness raising, meditation, and yoga. Hence, Gretchen's NISTs were prompting her to take on a sort of do-gooder-hippie value system. And this is how she presented herself. In fact, she was a vegan when I first met her.

But her *authentic* self was not concerned with the well-being of others or of the planet but with her own comfort, status, and financial well-being above all, at almost any cost. "Above all at…any cost" being the operative phrase here.

It is natural to look out for our own comfort and well-being; we all do so -- but not to the extent that Gretchen took it. Hers manifested in behaviors that were controlling, competitive, and generally lacking consideration for others. She even committed some small criminal acts, was caught in a few, and took pains to keep them off her teaching curriculum vitae.

Gretchen's actions were in such opposition to her public persona and her words that she confused those who were around her for any length of time. She would raise her voice to co-workers, unashamedly take credit for work others did, and betray the confidences of friends. And because she was simply exercising her authentic self, it was often without even realizing she was doing anything "'unacceptable.'" If confronted, she would shrug her shoulders, uncaring; she seemed to feel no remorse. Yet she knew enough to keep that outer persona of the New Age teacher out front and foremost. Guess I'd call it her NIST mask.

I do not know where Gretchen is today or how she is faring. I can only imagine how difficult it must be for a person like Gretchen to embrace her authentic self.

So how might we, the observer, consider the authentic self here? What was real? Was this person unable to confront and accept her true self? Was that the genesis of her NISTs? How did she integrate, in her own mind, those NISTs and her more dissonant behaviors? Did she even see the incongruities? Do any of us see *all* our own incongruities?

The disharmony Gretchen created began inside her and spread outward to others who expected A but experienced B. Can "a Gretchen" discard those NISTs and embrace that authentic self that is at odds with what the culture expects? An NIST in and of itself? What does an evolution of this type of authenticity look like?

A bit of a warning—we are social beings, interdependent in many ways, and if our authentic selves are strictly out for *only* self-survival, we are, as a species, in for a difficult time. Hence, we fear and demonize and label: narcissist, selfish, psychopath. And if one falls somewhere along that spectrum and is at the same time pretending—to oneself—to be otherwise, well, that is just crazy making for all in the vicinity.

What if the vicinity is planet Earth?

True Beauty *does* lie in authentic expression; its wideness and wildness—the infinite possibilities—are what has made True Beauty feared in the past, a target for oppression and suppression, a topic we will touch on later.

But for now let's assume that for most of us, the situation is not so extreme. For most of us, the gap between our authentic self and our presentation self isn't so troublesome. We have good bits, bad bits, lazy bits, and genius bits. The important bit is to take the time to meet and greet your authentic self and *all* its bits. It is the beginning of our lifelong evolution. Doing so makes the Way of Beauty much more accessible.

Philosophically and existentially speaking, there is no right or wrong. Circumstances are rarely black or white but the many gradients of gray in between. There are only guidelines as to how one may move most directly toward the inner peace and harmony that an awareness of personal authenticity brings, directing us toward the truly beautiful. If you are reading these pages, most likely you are on your way and have been for some time, whether the NISTs have sent you on some learning detours or not.

Another Story!

I write about personal authenticity with a lot of skin in that game, as they say. As a young woman, I wanted to go to art school. A large part of my authentic self was a maker, though I doubt I could have articulated it so succinctly at the time. I only knew whatever I felt inside fit most closely into the accepted moniker of "artist." Hence, art school.

My parents, the purse-string holders, adamantly refused to send me to art school. They felt I should have a more well-rounded education, get a liberal arts degree. Both my mother and my sister had gone to art school after high school. My mother said dismissively, with a loud sniff, "And look where it got us!" Well, I didn't think where they were was so bad, but then I *was* just seventeen.

Understand this happened in an era (mid-1960s), location, attitudes and circumstances that were very different from today. To go out and get one's own education loan was rare in the socioeconomic group in which I grew up. Parents were generally responsible for their children's education. Naïve as I was, such action was not even on my radar. In that time and place, I felt myself to be—and therefore was—dependent upon my parents for my education.

So, I took the only power I knew how to take: passive aggression. I refused to apply to any colleges. If I couldn't go to art school, I just wouldn't go anywhere.

Well, Mother was not to be outdone. She simply picked up the phone, made a few phone calls…and *boom!* I was enrolled and trucked off to a two-year junior college, a women's *finishing school* as they were called in those days. I knew I was supposed to find a husband along with my liberal arts degree.

After graduating from junior college, I went on to a secretarial school and learned to type and take shorthand, again at my mother's insistence. I understand now she was worried about how her epileptic daughter was going to earn a living, and I appreciate her concern. It was then, then, after all.

It was not the path I would have chosen in my young adulthood. My parents' considerations heavily overrode my nascent authentic self struggles within me. But, let's not oversimplify here: one real aspect of that young authentic self was timidity. I was not bold enough to figure out how to strike out on my own at that point. Conditioned in part by the experience of having seizures, *fear* made me timid, unsure. While it embarrasses me now (where is my self-compassion?), it was simply my truth then.

My need to create resurfaced, like a golden thread in the intricate tapestry of a life. At that somewhat creepy junior college, I took drawing and painting classes in addition to my regular course load. In the later years, I came home from secretarial jobs and made stained-glass windows in my basement, selling them at craft shows on weekends. I modeled for painters in exchange for oil-painting lessons.

I started running to alleviate my soul's anxiety and lose a few extra pounds. And my inner Maker used that experience to see a problem and create a solution: I invented the first sports bra, the Jogbra.

At that point, my life, my path took a dramatic detour that eventually led me to engage most fully my authentic self, but only once that detour into the business world was finished. For it wasn't actually a detour, but a long and challenging lesson about finding one's authentic self, and how to navigate through those shades of gray and keep one's integrity.

It led me to understand authentic beauty, True Beauty, and its importance.

To Practice and Hone One's Own Authenticity

1. In your journal, make a list of your behaviors and habits that aren't authentic. You probably already have a good idea about a few of them. How many of them grew out of NISTs? Note which NIST next to the inauthentic

Authenticity does not demand perfection, for if it did there would be no authentic people living on earth. Human beings embody contradictory values. Authenticity is that we embrace our incongruities and ambiguities while doing our best to make choices that reflect our core values.

–David Simon, The Ten Commitments

behavior. How many of your own "default settings" have you accepted and then never reviewed?

2. If you are unsure about an item, listen to that inner voice and feel that gut. An inauthentic energy feels askew; it doesn't sit right. If your reasoning/analytical mind seems to find justifications for a certain behavior or decision, fighting with your gut, this is a red flag. Pay attention! Add it to your list—no matter how much it seems like sacrilege!

3. Use your imagination and your journal to replace inauthentic behaviors with ones that reflect your true self and values. Allow yourself to be a little wild here, not hemmed in by convention! Just writing it down doesn't mean you have to actually do it or be it. You just have to *recognize yourself.* And, actually, some of these might surprise you by their pedestrian nature—and how easily they can unfold into your life. For me, one was that I love seeing the dawn, yet one of my less authentic behaviors getting in the way of this was a habit of getting too little sleep to rise early. I spent too many late evenings because of a stupid TV show or domestic chore that could have easily waited until the next day. To change the habit is just a matter of choice and discipline, not wild and crazy at all.

4. Envision the next chapter of your life and assure that the steps/choices you make align with that vision. I know this is no small thing, and how you do it is not as important as just simply doing it. A business consultant once told me early on in my business, "It doesn't matter if the plane is

off the ground, gaining altitude, and flying off and away if it doesn't know where it is going or what its destination is."

I got it. Where did I want this business to go? Was I going to build it to leave to my children? Or sell it and fund my retirement? Merge with another like company and keep going in perpetuity? The same is true of one's life. While our physical bodies all end up in the same final place, what do you want to experience on the way there? And with whom? So whether you create a vision board, create and update annual goals every New Year's Day, put an inspirational picture on the wall above your desk or meditation pillow...however you do it, do it. Consciously envision the next chapter of your life. And endeavor to have every major step you take be in alignment with that vision.

Years later, I learned my early business consultant had been paraphrasing Lucius Seneca: "If one does not know to which port one is sailing, no wind is favorable." And so ancient wisdom finds application in our modern Western business culture.

5. Look at the material world you've created around yourself. Does it align with your core values? If you are fortunate enough, find the balance between abundance and simplicity. Identify and list the fears that are helping to maintain scarcity in certain areas of your field. Just spotting and acknowledging them to yourself can help defray anxiety levels. Fear is the number-one reason we hold ourselves back. It suffocates our authenticity.

6. Because this practice may initiate some changes in your daily life, practice all of the above with compassion for those around you. Remember that True Beauty is and facilitates harmony, not discord. Smooth the transitions when possible; let those you care for know what you are endeavoring to do. Your aspiration to live a more authentic life may well inspire them to do the same. Everything is in relationship!

Simply put, practicing authenticity is working on "to thine own self be true." Because here is the thing: if you don't tell yourself your truth, you're automatically lying to everyone else, too.

Yet stay aware: as shown in the be wary of the truth practice, truth is not static. *Your* truth is not static. Being true and accessing your authenticity is about being sensitive to life's cycles.

And here is a bit of wisdom: the energy put into maintaining a false self is far greater than the energy it takes to start honoring and maintaining one's authentic self. In the end, *being* one's real self takes little effort—you don't have to *think* so much about it! The transition to starting up and getting into that authentic state is what can be difficult.

So it is too bad; we are not all perfect people and 100 percent truly beautiful—and you know by now I am not talking the tabloid version of beauty here. But we can strive to be beauty, and in so doing, we are actually *practicing* beauty. We can strive to add harmony rather than discord into the energy of our personal universe(s). And yes, all this takes practice.

Creativity, affluence, and serenity are the offspring of the practice of authenticity. It will take time, but it's well worth it.

Your time is limited, so don't waste
it living someone else's life.
Don't be trapped by dogma—which is living
with the results of other people's thinking.
Don't let the noise of others' opinions
drown out your own inner voice.
And most important, have the courage
to follow your heart and intuition.
They somehow already know what you truly
want to become. Everything else is secondary.

—Steve Jobs, 2005 Stanford University commencement address

VIII. Practice Dynamic Acceptance of Self

Our deepest fear is not that we are inadequate. Our deepest fear is that we are powerful beyond measure. It is our light not our darkness that most frightens us.

—MARIANNE WILLIAMSON

I FIND SELF-ACCEPTANCE one of the most rigorous and difficult practices. Acceptance of myself and my own limitations, as well as my strengths, has been an ongoing challenge. Yet I don't think I'm alone; I'm guessing this is true for many.

Practicing self-acceptance is closely linked to having compassion for ourselves, as we realize and become, consciously, our wondrous, nonperfect, authentic selves. That's a mouthful! Such self-acceptance doesn't happen overnight. Just as we have to spend time learning about what makes us authentically us, so too it takes time to accept that self.

I recently heard a teacher, Deborah Grassman from Opus Peace (see Further Reading section), exclaim, "Who teaches us how to fail? Who teaches us how to lose? Yet we all do!" Her point was that there are rich and deep lessons in each failure, each loss, and we are not encouraged or directed on how to make the most of these personal and unique-to-us gems of wisdom. Rather than be ashamed or only in grief around these inevitable life events, accepting and integrating them into our knowledge base is both useful and an important building block of dynamic and compassionate self-acceptance.

A Story

By middle school, I was intensely uninterested in gym classes. Perhaps many girls were; I know my best friend disliked those structured, competition-oriented PE classes too. I loved being outdoors, swimming in the ocean, and climbing trees, but not those dank locker rooms and whistle-blowing gym instructors!

But there were the "jock" girls who relished gym and understood the rules of field hockey, were eager to get out on the tennis courts, and always seemed to get along with the gym teacher. They intimidated me. Somehow, it seemed to me, I was *less* than them because I didn't get the whole sporty competitive thing. When possible, my friend and I opted for Beginning Bowling as our gym class choice.

Growing up, my mother, in her wisdom, would intone: "Horses sweat, men perspire, women *glow*."

I didn't even like to glow. Not in a locker room, anyway.

So avoiding gym classes, doing some body surfing in the summer ocean, and walking everywhere was my idea of sports.

Until I discovered the meditation of running…and my world changed.

My body and I became friends. The body that all my life had regularly betrayed me with sudden, violent convulsions now was the glorious entity that freed me to move and travel over the ground. We glowed, we sweated, and we gloried. We sang down the trails and over the streets.

My running was never competitive. Quite the opposite. Running reconnected me to the natural world—put me back into it and became one of my first spiritual practices. It is totally ironic, frankly, that this practice spawned my financial success and exposure to the grit of the competitive business world.

When I first started running, I was trying to jog around an indoor track—a whole quarter mile. I was very out of shape, and it was hard on my body and my self-esteem. I felt like such a failure! I tried not to notice all those others who easily swept by me and around that track several times without seeming to even break a sweat.

It took me weeks, but the day I actually made it all the way around I felt like I'd won an Olympic medal! I was so proud of myself! Then the day came that I made it around four times, without stopping or walking. A mile! It taught me the value of perseverance, the lesson born from the earlier failures.

Fast forward a few years and many logged miles to my invention of the sports bra and creation of a business around it. Being clear that the Jogbra was athletic equipment, not lingerie, I knew (really, gnew) it had to be sold in sporting goods stores. Sporting goods stores! I'd hardly ever set foot in one! In fact, until taking my bra into those stores to sell it, I had entered one only to buy my running shoes. The sporting goods industry was as foreign and intimidating to the woman I had become as those long-ago gym classes were to my girlhood self.

One day, back in 1990 or so, I found myself at a very large national sporting goods show. My company was quite successful by then. I recall walking around the noisy, people-filled show taking in aisle after aisle lined with booths selling everything from athletic clothing to fishing rods and baseball bats. Every athletic shoe manufacturer was there. The place was a bustling mosaic of color, people, and commerce.

And I wondered, how the hell had I ended up here? I felt like a complete fraud, with nothing in common with all these enthusiastic jocks and jockettes. It seemed to me that the glorification of sports competition and the glitz and noise that went along with it had so little to do with my love of a quiet run through the woods. Or with my aspiring artist self. The choices that brought me here had made sense at the time, I'd thought....

The irony was not lost on me. *Is* not lost on me. An important aspect of my authentic self, the runner, had spawned this persona of sporting goods queen. "Sports Bra Maven" follows me to this day. How could I accept this aspect, a very public and time-consuming aspect, of the self I had become?

The further irony is that I no longer can be that runner. In the late eighties, both my knees blew out, first one and then the other. I had to give up running altogether. And I *still* miss it. Often, when I see a runner, I will feel again that sensation, the wondrous gestalt of the running experience.

I learned a great deal about myself and something about the world during those Jogbra years simply by dealing with the incongruities of my authentic self and attempting the everyday work of self-acceptance. I say "simply." Truth is that I could come to accept myself and what I was doing for two very real and authentic (for me) reasons.

The first was that I believed in the need and the necessity of the product that I was selling. That it made sense to sell it in a milieu that was foreign to me was just something I had to learn to deal with.

The second was that I had to be responsible for myself, and that meant both financially as well as medically. By the time I founded the Jogbra Company, I had experienced the stigma and discrimination that came as a direct result of having epilepsy. And it very much existed in the employment field as well as elsewhere.

By starting my own business, I was employing myself, and by being my own boss, I could circumvent many of the health-related obstacles I had previously encountered. I had, on a deep and real level, accepted something I could not change and come up with a solution to secure my financial well-being. It worked.

Going into business? Into the *sporting goods* business? I gnow and know that although seemingly incongruous with that girl in gym class and that young woman runner, as difficult as it was for that learn-as-I-go entrepreneur—I am better for it. And in learning so much about myself in that endeavor, what appeared a detour from my spiritual and artistic path, I came to respect myself, accept myself, and believe in myself so much more than did that timid young woman who graduated from an innocuous junior college, engagement ring in hand, way back when.

And funny how that abhorred secretarial training came in handy too!

Evolution. That word again—it is why this practice is about *dynamic* acceptance of oneself. The word *dynamic* means a process that is in constant change and progress. We cannot ever look in the mirror and say, "OK, I accept me warts and all; I'm done!" unless we do it virtually *every* day from the vantage point of our own evolving spirits, our evolving culture, and our evolving world—and using the yardstick of True Beauty.

The Importance of the Practice

What role does self-acceptance have in the reclaiming of True Beauty into our sensibility and culture? This: the more accepting and loving we are of ourselves, the more accepting and compassionate we tend to be of others, no matter what differences we may perceive in them.

Then, also, there is often the gap between what one feels *capable* of versus what we perceive as *having actually accomplished.* This gap can feel great, depending on our expectations. Now lay our NISTs on the top of that, and the subsequent self-disappointment and self-punishment can all too often make self-acceptance a prized achievement rather than a natural outcome of an achievement.

We also live in an odd era where, on one hand, the ego is supreme and "looking out for no. 1" is celebrated, while on the other hand, only a very few are good *enough.* We constantly compare ourselves to a few who we've raised up in adulation, sometimes for no apparent reason (think tabloid cover photo fodder here). Are we as smart, as thin, as young, as fast, as talented…the key word being "as."

Our appreciation of our own uniqueness and abilities and talents—what makes us authentic—is all too often lost in an unrelenting sea of "compare and contrast." We have fallen out of the True Beauty lifeboat of both/and.

Yet in promoting self-acceptance, I do not want to suggest or imply complacency. As in all things, really, there is a balance to be struck between acceptance and improvement. Acceptance doesn't have to mean "resignation" or "unchanging"—rather, to see oneself as clearly as is possible and embrace what is seen *lovingly.* If there is a part of the self in that embrace that could use some tweaking, needs some care, or that you would just like to improve, then do so. For this last part, I think of my desire to improve and increase my mastery in art techniques.

Part of my journey of self-acceptance is accepting that I have epilepsy, a condition with no cure. This multifaceted limitation has presented itself in many different ways. I do *not* accept that all the presenting limitations cannot be worked around. There are ways I can and have "improved my lot," as the saying goes.

Yet I have accepted that the self, myself, must endure certain limitations and circumstances; it pains ocean-loving me that I can never scuba dive. There have been times in my life when I have not been able or allowed to drive a car. How this illness presents itself varies, so predictability—even day to day—is rare. Virtually all my life I've taken medication every day and live with that medication's side effects (one trades one problem for another, hopefully lesser, problem). Others have their own ideas and fixed opinions about what epilepsy is; some choose not to include me in their lives.

So, how can one acknowledge *this* is my current reality, *this* is who I am, and, *now, how* can I move forward? Indeed, how to find the harmony point between lovingly embracing critical self-appraisal, acceptance, and self-improvement? It is in this practice of *dynamic self-acceptance.* It helps to sidestep those insidious forms of denial and self-deception that can facilitate a false form of self-acceptance and blinkered self-esteem.

To Practice Dynamic Acceptance of Self

1. Contemplate the work you've done and are doing on being your authentic self. It is easier to accept ourselves when we are embracing the authentic self. If you keep a journal, please start incorporating this line of thinking—authenticity and the progression of your self-acceptance—into your notes. Notice those things,

essential though they may be in this moment, that are not quite on your purpose...what can you do to start steering yourself toward greater authenticity?

2. Take care of your body. Notice where you are resisting such care and make a plan to confront this. To get to your plan, have a dialog with yourself. Here is an example:

   I am one of those women who has a closet full of different-sized clothes depending on this year's body size. I am not accepting of this; I know it is unhealthy for my body weight to swing up and down. When I gain weight, it affects my overall health and how I physically feel on a daily basis. I go through periods of resistance in terms of actually taking action on this, which leads to my being disappointed in myself.

   Am I being true to myself? Authentic? My body—my joints, my lymphatic system, and my cardiovascular network—all are virtually yelling at me, and I'm just putting those needs at the bottom of my list of priorities. Why? Is there an emotional component I am not paying attention to? Honoring? Is there an environmental issue? Is there some old truth hanging on that is having a physical effect?

   In reviewing and answering my questions to myself, I may spot the emotional upheaval that has left me not only eating poorly, but my body is also producing massive amounts cortisol, which has resulted in weight gain. Now I have choices based in a level of consciousness.

   A dialog such as this between you and you is just one example of how the process of *dynamic* self-acceptance can start to take place.

3. Self-acceptance in failure: Think of a *failure* as just another word for *rehearsal.* Don't beat yourself up and then give up. Trial and error is the way of artists and scientists. Be fully present with the choices that are available, and continue forward. Persevere!

4. In dealing with others, remember: everyone is doing his or her best from their own point of view and level of awareness—including you.

5. When necessary, *forgive*—especially yourself.

   The concept of forgiveness can be difficult. I never really got it until I heard the following very succinct definition: "To forgive is to give up, let go, and then move on!" *Give up...and let go.* Way easier said than done. Me, give up? That competitive facet of me didn't want to do it. Then, having given up and truly let go—to keep moving forward, cleanly, with no residual resentments or regrets? A tall order in some instances.

   You know you have truly let go when you no longer even remember the offense!

   But the ability to forgive is a natural outcome of practicing True Beauty. One cannot be aware of true, deep beauty in all things, in ourselves, and be unable to forgive. Of course, like all of this, it takes practice; it *is* a practice. And I am suggesting that we start with ourselves—because often that is the most difficult act of forgiving. And we have the chance every day!

Dynamic self-acceptance might be one of the more difficult beauty practices—we can be so tough on ourselves or so blind.

But, it is also integral and necessary. We have the chance to practice dynamic self-acceptance every moment of every day.

One of the seldom-mentioned keys to
the spiritual life is acceptance.
Not acceptance of others but of ourselves. So
often we focus on what we want to change…
lessen our character defects…What
if we are acceptable even
in the times we have difficulty accepting ourselves?…
The poet Theodore Roethke…tells us: "in
a dark time, the eye begins to see."

—Julia Cameron

IX. Practice Cultivating Harmonic Relationships

Relationships are all there is. Everything in the universe only exists because it is in relationship to everything else. Nothing exists in isolation. We have to stop pretending we are individuals that can go it alone.

—Margaret Wheatley

Relationship relates to beauty first in terms of what a deep, long, complicated, yet universal history we as a species have created with language and the communication arts in our pursuit of relationship creation.

Second, it is integral in how we perceive and process information, both verbally and nonverbally. Third, it is in how we then attach *value* to the information based on our complete or incomplete understanding of it, and finally, how we express and share that information and its perceived value. Look at all the relationship flows involved in the above list!

What is meant by "relationship"? At its most basic, it is the existence of communication between an entity and itself or between two separate entities. It can be felt and perceived by others outside the relationship, but need not be in order to exist. Our cosmos is in endless relationship—with itself, as it is self-organizing—as well as with all else. Whether we name it autopoiesis, holarchy, love, gravity, entropy, or strange attractors, we are naming a type and form of relationship. Harmony is when relationships are in synchronous flow. Discord is when relationships are flowing against one another: intention and counterintention.

True Beauty is the outcome of the existence of harmony. In fact, a classical Greek definition of beauty, preferred by Aristotle and paraphrased by Rollo May, is, "Beauty is the condition when everything fits…when one has the conviction that nothing could be added or subtracted. All the parts are in harmony with all the other parts."

And if we truly grasp and accept that everything is in relationship at all times—all energies, all matter, time, space, fields, my optimism, skepticism—then we begin to see the importance of paying attention to beauty's bountiful presence flowing around us. Yes, it is punctuated with its opposite—the yang in the yin, the light piercing the dark, and vice versa. Which will we choose to accentuate? To nurture? To replicate in our daily living?

What relationships will we choose?

A further aspect of my definition of True Beauty is this: beauty is harmonious relationships. It is first and foremost in relationship with itself, finding harmony with itself, then with the other(s).

OK. What relationships? Well—*all relationships.* Beauty is harmonious relationship in and between people, between places, between people and objects—in fact, between all matter, energy, space, time, and perhaps even the nonlocal as my friends in physics might suggest.

While there are gradients of beauty, it is an essential state of being that is a continuum. Harmony and discord are "complementary colors" on this wheel, each having its place in creating a beautiful, balanced world, and therefore each is beauty-full.

Therein lies the paradox that I propose is the energy engine of the universe. It is also why holding that eponymous attitude of the Both/And Universe Practice is so essential to finding and maintaining harmony.

To practice cultivating harmonious relationships is, in fact, to be and practice True Beauty.

As with the word *beauty*, the words *harmony* and *relationship* also have become overused and thus often misunderstood. Simply, harmony means "fits together."

Following the path of True Beauty is in great part about noticing, cultivating, and sustaining harmonious relationship. While relationship begins first between you and you (remember the practice of being our authentic selves), the next most important and primary relationship is between you and the "other"—really, a series of others" whose main characteristic is that they are perceived as external of the "me."

While there is the "other" of our immediate environment, our first "other of flesh" is probably family, the one you are born into and then the one you choose and create beyond that. Third, of course, are all the relationships you choose to create just between folks and other species (think pets and, say, houseplants).

Though this may all seem obvious, looking at the status of today's family; community life; ecology; and abused, abandoned, and mass-produced animals—it isn't. We have only to look around to see the growing anomie in our culture.

Animus Mundi

When speaking to others about the concept that everything has a soul (*animus mundi*), I sometimes get the quasi question, "So, you must be vegan or vegetarian?"

Beauty is the synergistic, flowing field that holds all in dynamic, resonating harmony as the next movement unfurls.

I am not. I am a meat eater. But I am no longer a mindless meat eater. I do not eat meat every day or even every week. When I do, I thank the animal that gave its life to sustain mine. I decry the mass-producing beef/chicken/egg/dairy facilities and do my best to avoid their products. The very least I can do is vote with my dollar, consumer that I am.

Animals are not objects. Animals should (yes, *that* word) not be bred/produced as if they are merely products for our consumption. This practice, in fact, I label as ugly; it is not anywhere on the True Beauty continuum.

And, by the way, I do not leave out plant material I consume when saying my thanks. This small thanking act is acknowledging and respecting those ensouled others who are doing me—and all of us—a *great* service. It is the way of our natural world, this exchange. That does not mean that it need be cruel, unfeeling, or mindless.

Caution: we are none of us perfect, and those of us in North America are living in an age of amazing plentitude. While being aware and making conscious choices when you can, do not beat yourself up when the best choice or action isn't possible. (You and the kids and their friends are at the stadium and they all want hot dogs and burgers? Well, OK.) The economics of this issue assures that change in this venue will be slow. As long as we are doing what we can, we are practicing True Beauty.

Perhaps not oddly, *relationship* is a word that has been so overused in our culture today as to almost be meaningless. Businesses now have "relationship brokers" in place of customer-service departments. We don't have friendships, love affairs, or acquaintances anymore. We have relationships with everything imaginable. And this would not be entirely wrongheaded if we were not so often inured to what relationship really means, really requires. Perhaps the word has become overused in a kind of reactive attempt to disguise the weakened state of our social relationships and communities.

A Story?

There is no *one* story to tell of relationships. There are millions. Every culture is full of them because almost every story revolves around relationship, doesn't it? Think for a moment. The Bible tells of many relationships: Adam and Eve, Cain and Abel, David and Goliath, and of course most centrally, God and humankind. All of Shakespeare's work revolves around relationship antics and misunderstandings. Comic book heroes are in relationship with crime, justice, and the "American way" (to quote the voice-over in the 1950s *Superman* TV show).

A science-themed book I recently read explores the relationship between bodies in the universe—stars, star clusters, galaxies, and supergalaxies, and posits the probability of more far-flung relationships. Math is about relationships between numbers and the effect they can have upon one another. There are all the stories about humanity and nature, girls and boys, plants and pests, machines and tools, people and tools, horses and cowboys, gods and goddesses…

I could go on and on, but the quote at the beginning of this chapter says it all: everything is in relationship to everything else. Stories highlight particulars of certain relationships. Sitting here writing this, a zillion unseen air molecules are bumping into each other and bumping into my skin, like a wild scene of bumper cars. The whole universe, actually, is like that. And depending upon the relationships, membrane permeability, and a few other things, it's not only bumping and bouncing off that's going on but melding, attaching, integrating, and splitting.

Everything is about relationship. Conflict occurs when one intention, one motion meets a counterintention or an opposite motion. Resonance and harmony occur when separate entities meet and flow together, when they find the notes that allow them to sing in tune and flow together, perhaps combining to create something other.

The Importance of the Practice

Relationship is about attraction and resonance—being attractive, *attracted,* and resonating with another, only to find upon entering into the dance of relationship that one plus one equals not two but three—and we are not talking about baby here. Rather, that somehow the attraction of the two has created something bigger than the separate single units apart: the "field of attraction" is the observable energy created by and between the two. Gravity is a field of attraction. You could say, quite literally, that the moon fell for the earth. We are drawn to and enter into a relationship with what- or whomever we are attracted to. When there is a resonance—a reverberation and return of said attraction—we are actually in relationship with the other.

Millions of books have been written and therapies developed to help create healthy and happy relationships. At day and experts' end, it all boils down to what is of true importance to you.

And having figured that out, what is your *order* of importances, your priorities? To what and where do we give our time, energy, and attention? How much goes to ourselves, to the job, the sports, the maintenance of possessions, and to the journey of others around us? On what do we *focus?* Remember the Authentic Self Practice? Once we are truly ourselves and not just doing the NIST dance, we will be able to easily, naturally harmonize with others.

Or not.

The opposite of attraction is repulsion, like magnets, you know. But *repulsion* is a strong word—the scientific word, really, and not what I want to convey here. In relationships we might say, "There wasn't a spark" or "I just didn't get her" or some such. There is no judgment in this reaction if it is coming from a place of discernment and workability for oneself and *not* from a place of criticism. Remember, this is about being in sync with, in tune with. It is about building, creating, and nurturing.

Yet this is also not about sameness. Often we seek those who have something—a trait, a talent, an ability—we don't possess. It might be a comfort with adventure, an ease with mathematics, or an ability to grow things. This difference can be just the thing that completes the resonating tone in the duet.

And, then, there is this big question: can we accept the care, love, and concern of another flowing to us? We often hear of the joys of giving. But how many of us are comfortable with receiving? How is it to be the subject of another's focus? How hard is it to simply smile and say "thank you" when someone does a thoughtful thing or pays us a compliment?

What we may think of as personal relationships are not irrelevant or extracurricular. They are the source of the central expression of harmony, of a life of True Beauty. In formally entering—that is, consciously choosing—a relationship with another human being, we are entering the dance and mystery of the universe itself.

Later we will see how being in conscious relationship with all things, not just our fellow humans, augments the Way of True Beauty because remember, it is a core premise of the Way of Beauty that, in fact, *all* is in relationship, not just human to human, or even man to his dog. *All* is in relationship *all* the time. Being in conscious relationship, therefore, is a tall order.

The Importance of Communication in Relationships

I cannot relegate effective communication to just a practice for nurturing harmonic relationships. Communication is integral to relationship. It is difficult, in fact, to separate the two.

My definition of communication is not restricted to the spoken word. Movement, gesture, facial expression, a glance—all these send messages; all these are communications.

Let's look at the notion of living life as if in dialog. For if we are all in relationship with all, all the time, then we are in dialog all the time. Right? Hang in there with me.

"Dialog" as I mean it is David Bohm's definition. Bohm suggested that conflict could be avoided and harmony maintained if, when people came together to discuss and share, they could take a position but hold it with nonattachment, an objectivity that allows one to suspend judgment with the intention to broaden knowledge and creativity. Very important that: the intention to broaden knowledge.

I had always thought of this more as a way of being, really, which turns out to be what Bohm was really suggesting in *Wholeness and the Implicate Order*: "If [man] thinks of the totality as constituted of independent fragments, then that is how his mind will tend to operate, but if he can include everything coherently and harmoniously in an overall whole that is undivided, unbroken, and without a border then his mind will tend to move in a similar way, and from this will flow an orderly action within the whole."

In my best moments, I strive to live *life* as such a dialog. In other words, unattached to any one point of view, deeply listening to the other, open to all points of view without having to "have it" or "take it on" or be "right," and at the same time be response-able—able to respond, hopefully with the greatest good in mind. And for me, here's the trick: I strive at the same time to *also* be aware of my own preferences and choices so as to be responsible for my own condition in as much as I am consciously able to make authentic-to-me decisions, to always be aware of the eternal energy of True Beauty, supporting it, nurturing it, and acknowledging it.

This is the closest to a personal credo I have articulated in recent times. I wish I succeeded at it more often. I am learning to forgive myself for my failures. I am learning to consider them my rehearsals.

Consider how you communicate. How effective are you at both expressing yourself and listening to others within your field of attraction? Outside of that field? Effective communication is the key to authentic, successful relationships.

To Practice Harmonic Relationship

1. Remember to practice the Golden Rule. It may be trite, but it's oh so true! Know that you are in relationship with all around you all the time. Your energy affects the energy field of that and those around you.

2. If you have not already, educate yourself about mass-production food practices (dairy, egg, beef, and chicken are big ones). This will give you the oomph you may need to create a deeper relationship with your food. You may even change some eating habits. It was the one about the beef industry that did it for me.

   In consideration that your meat and vegetables were once living entities, at each meal and snack, thank the food for giving its life to sustain yours. This needn't be fancy or protracted, just sincere. If your family says grace at meals, add this simple phrase in!

   For those lucky enough to be able to grow their own vegetables, you already know/gnow you have a relationship with those plants. Don't disregard it. Let them know you are raising them to bring to your table, and send them your loving gratitude every time you are in the garden with them. I bet they will respond! Every life has purpose; you are sharing theirs with them. Consider planting a bit more than you need to allow some to go to seed and feed the birds or the insects or, eventually, the soil that the plant will return to.

3. Make a list of those people, places, things that are very important to you. This is a big clue to your own

attractions and resonances. Look at this list again with an eye toward how it supports or detracts from creating harmony in your life. For instance, if you are passionate about the ocean but live in Nebraska, you might want to think about that. Are you in a harmonic relationship with where you live?

4. Make another list of what you want to include in your life and see *more* of in the world. If you focus on the negative, it is the negative that will occupy your world. So focus on what you would prefer to have in residence! Review this list periodically during the year. How are you doing? Add and subtract as per your authentic self's voice. No one ever said your authentic self is static. Be aware and share your awareness in your relationships.

5. Nurture the "higher companions" in your life, and be one to others. A higher companion is one who inspires, supports, and encourages…and everyone smiles and laughs a lot when he or she is around!

6. Receive others' communications graciously. When someone gives you a compliment, notice your first mental reaction. Is it, "Oh no, this old thing?" Or "Must be insincere; I can do better! Really!" Sometimes we even say as much. I've certainly heard myself saying, "Uh oh, well this old painting/dress/floral arrangement was really just something I threw together." A response like this actually *invalidates* the compliment giver. Just say, "Thank you."

7. On the other hand, if someone makes a rather snarky remark that is either an outright insult or could be taken as one, practice smiling through it. If it needs to be considered or processed, do it later when removed from the incident. Remember, it is *your* body that is impacted by your responses, whether they be pleasurable, happy, anxiety ridden, or angry.

Consider the following. We humans are social beings.
We come into the world as the result of others' actions.
We survive here in dependence on others.
Whether we like it or not, there is hardly a moment
of our lives when we do not benefit
from others' activities.
For this reason it is hardly surprising that
most of our happiness arises in the context
of our relationships with others.
—HH Dalai Lama

X. Follow The K.I.S.S. Method

Simplicity is about subtracting the obvious and adding the meaningful.

—John Maeda

"Keep it simple, sweetie," or K.I.S.S., was originally introduced into popular culture with the second S standing for "stupid." It is modified here to remove that snide sting.

I want to be clear about my language and intent here. By "simple" I do not mean simplistic. Nor am I suggesting any sort of dumbing down of your activities, style, communication—or anything. Probably quite the opposite.

Think of *this* simplicity this way: what is the *essence*? In a communication, in a task, in whatever life dishes up that day, what is the essence of what needs to be accomplished, experienced, or expressed? Ask yourself this before elaborating beyond the essential elegance that is the simplicity. Then go forward.

"Elegance" is key here. This is not the same simplicity concept of "bare necessity" as in Puritanical thought—not at all! Remember, this is a *beauty* practice. Elegance, like graciousness or kindness, is not dictated by monetary wealth. It is not synonymous with any decorative style or preference. The dictionary definition of elegance is "the quality of being graceful and stylish in appearance or manner"; or "the quality of being pleasingly ingenious and simple." In the practice of True Beauty, it is the second definition we are primarily referencing.

In this context, we want to understand simplicity not as the opposite of complexity but as the essence of a complexity. Think about that for a moment: simplicity is the *essence* of a complexity.

And do not confuse *confusion* with complexity. They are not even in the same family! Confusion may be the result of encountering a complexity we have not yet wrestled to the ground, so to speak—but do not confuse (ha ha) one with the other. Confusion, in fact, is our first clue that there is an underlying complexity of which we are not yet the mistress. We may, in fact, be missing the essential simplicity that is at the core.

A Simple Little Story

When I moved into my house, I ordered what I thought to be a smallish chandelier to go over the dining room table. It came to me carefully packed—in parts. Gracefully arched arms amputated from the lamp's central body, and dozens of little crystal dangly things that had to be put together and then paired to the correct arm that itself had dozens of other slightly larger crystal dangly things needing to be correctly hung that then had to be connected to the correct larger arm that had to be connected to the...you get the picture. A potential nightmare.

After I was done with my, er, *amazement* that it had been sent to me in all these pieces, I practiced my two-minute smile drill, remembered that I *like* puzzles, and sat down with it spread all around me. What was the essence of this task? To find pieces that went together until I had a completed chandelier. And no one but me had any deadline in mind. I put on some music and got started....

Beauty plus simplicity equals elegance:
the True Beauty K.I.S.S. equation.

Several days, cups of coffee, glasses of wine, and help from a friend (hanging it so that the last round of crystal dangly things could be affixed) I did have, whew!, a chandelier over my dining room table.

I know it well.

And yes, I realized I could have made a more simple overhead lighting choice!

To Practice Keeping It Simple

1. Take a moment to suss out the essence of the task or experience at hand.

2. Relax; allow it to be easy (for instance in the story above, floor, music, and release of having any specific time frame). Too often, I find that I allow my anxiety about the *potential* complexity of a problem to actually create additional difficulty to any real difficulty of the task at hand. Relaxing and presupposing ease, eases!

3. Be present. For me this requires letting go of any lurking intentions or desires that are not connected to the task at hand. *Being present is being committed.*

Practicing simplicity is very much about noticing and responding with awareness and elegance. Too often I think we anticipate (the worry factor) that things will be more complicated

Simplicity is the ultimate sophistication.

–Leonardo da Vinci

than they are or need to be. Remember, simplicity is the essence of a complexity.

Really, so many things can be simple, sweetie!

XI. Practice Creation

When imagination is allowed to move to deep places, the sacred is revealed.

—Thomas Moore, *Care of the Soul*

Being productive. Think about it: we are quite *content* and *intent* when we are creating. I might be so bold as to say we are never happier than when we are creating—what I have come to gnow as joining in the generative, creative vibrations of the universe.

The spirit of creation flows to and through us in many ways, waves, and forms. To create is to participate in the process of creation that is actually occurring everywhere, always. Such is the song and work/play of the universe. The act of creation is not just for artists and gods.

We are *all* able to participate in the act of creation. Whatsoever and wherever your generative urge pushes you, calls you to create, go there, do it. Build an engine, sew, paint; make dinner, art, or furniture. Have and raise children; nurture other people's children. Care for animals. Knit. Tend a garden. Build sandcastles along the shore. Make music. Repair and refurbish. Tear down and then rebuild. See a need? Invent its solution.

You don't have to be an artist to create. The act of creating is not just about making stuff. I believe we are all artists and artisans as we are painting our lives, building relationships, forging jobs, and planning for our families. All that's needed to practice creating is a willingness to look, *really* look, with the intention of seeing what is there, not only with the eyes but with the heart, the usual senses, and with one's intuition. *See!*

The next step that turns seeing into creating is our further willingness to give in to that desire we feel—do you know it?—to *respond* in some manner, to interact with what we are perceiving. To engage with it, change it, spice it up, or water it down. Often, we are moved to replicate a beauty we have identified in our surroundings—which is still creating. We plant flowers, cut them, and bring them inside; smell good food cooking and go home and make a meal; hear someone whistling a tune and start singing ourselves.

A Story

I was so excited to learn of the Navajo concept of *hózhó*. It is the kernel of The Way of Beauty, yet it has no equivalent in the English language. It is the seed from the "heritage plant" for the new paradigm, one that we must plant in the compost of our decaying culture in order to reap the beauty of justice, harmony, and balance of continual creation.

I was not aware of the Diné (as the Navajo people refer to themselves) culture when I first started thinking about the importance of True Beauty. When I came upon it in my research for this book, I was astounded to say the least. I was not crazy; others have known too!

Difficult to translate, hózhó is at the core of the Navajo essence, a definitively beauty-centric culture. Hózhó embodies, represents, and expresses all that is good according to the Diné. It is such a broad, all-pervasive, and basic concept, coloring so much of the Diné culture and philosophy that it actually made the need for some words—like *religion* and *art*—nonexistent. It covers what we think of as beauty, harmony, blessing, order, success, health, and goodness.

I believe we must emulate this Diné philosophy to better shift away from the current paradigm driving our modern Western culture and start birthing a twenty-first-century version of hózhó because, of course, the values of the hózhó culture were aligned with authentic beauty.

Gary Witherspoon, a professor emeritus at the University of Washington and author of *Language and Art in the Navajo Universe*, has spent quite a lot of time with the Navajo and written extensively about their art and culture. To understand what a beauty-centric society might look like and how it might function, I strongly suggest reading his book.

In the meantime, to clarify the important hózhó concept, a few excerpts are here:

> Hózhó refers to the holistic environment and to the universal dimension of beauty, harmony, and well-being...The Navajo metaphor envisions a universe where the primary orientation is directed toward the maintenance or the restoration of hózhó. Hózhó means "beauty" or "beautiful conditions." But this is a term that means much more than beauty...[it] expresses the intellectual notion of order, the emotional state of happiness, the physical state of health, the moral condition of good, and the aesthetic dimension of harmony.

> The Navajo do not look for beauty; they normally find themselves engulfed in it. When it is disrupted, they restore it; when it is lost or diminished, they renew it; when it is present, they celebrate it...The Navajo express and celebrate this "beauty" in speech and prayer, in song and dance, in myth and ritual, and in their daily lives and activities, as well as in their graphic arts. Art, therefore, is not divorced from subsistence, science, philosophy, or theology but is an integral part of both common activities and cosmic schemes.
>
> Hózhó is the grand metaphor by which the Navajo understand the world and their place within it.

Now this is a societal architecture I would be happy to inhabit! One in which making is a natural and sacred act—considered participation in the ongoing creation of the universe itself.

In a very essential way, the Diné illustrate True Beauty and its practice, The Way of True Beauty, because for them beauty is *not* in the eye of the beholder as much as it's in the mind of its creator and in the creator's relationship to that which has been created. Relationship again, of course!

This is why the issue of taste as we know and engage in it today becomes virtually irrelevant. Beauty is a very personal endeavor, experience, and adventure—much like personal growth.

The Diné did what I am strongly suggesting we must do: generate beauty within ourselves and project it upon the universe. Create the beauty.

The Navajo say *shi/l hózhó*, or "with me there is beauty," *shii' hózhó*, or "in me there is beauty," and *shaa hózhó*, or "from me beauty radiates."

In our Western world's dominant cultural paradigm beauty is, in essence, static; that is, it is something to be observed, maintained and preserved. Our, idea of beauty has become an unchanging formula. True Beauty is dynamic, alive. It is not a static, rigid *thing.*

Why does it matter, this fluidity versus rigidity? Because it means we all have the opportunity to create anew. We are not helpless. We need not be hopeless. We have a choice to create True Beauty in response to gloom, doom, and ugliness. Pollyanna? Sign me up!

A Navajo often counts his wealth in the songs he knows and especially in the songs he has created. A poor Navajo is one who has no songs, for songs enrich one's experiences and beautify one's activities.

Here is one of my favorite observations from Gary Witherspoon's work: "In white society it is the exceptional and abnormal person that becomes an artist. The artist is usually associated with marginality and nonconformity with regard to the mainstream of society. From this marginal position the artist dedicates himself almost solely to his artistic creations. The nonartist among the Navajo is a rarity. Moreover, Navajo artists integrate their artistic endeavors into their other activities. Living is not a way of art for them, but art is a way of living."

The Importance of the Practice

While creating and making are always sacred acts, they are also daily, mundane, and essential acts. Herein lies its wonderful paradox. In beauty practice, we must remove the preciousness or elitist attitudes from art and artistry while restoring its essential-to-well-being role in our very nature.

Might we imagine a version of this in our world? What if we, too, measured a person's wealth by the number of songs he or she contributed? Well, that's probably not going to happen soon...unless you are the Beatles or Mozart.

What if a business was not measured primarily by its fiscal health alone, but other measurements were *equally as important*—such as, how satisfied both its customers *and* its employees are; how much service and/or pro bono work it provides annually; its environmental impact; its ROA (return on *aesthetics* as well as ROI are concepts we'll explore later).

What if greed made no sense? What if harmony and beauty were the conditions for which one strived, for which *everyone* strived? What if the well-being of those around us was as important as our own well-being?

It is not impossible.
It is not impossible.
Practice True Beauty.

Being creative has little to do with talent in the way that we understand that word today and more to do with talent in the sense of having a feeling for something, a predisposition for an ability and our inherent need to express our responses to our world. It also has much to do with curiosity and learning, need and solution, conviction and generativity. And, of course, it has to do with True Beauty—the need to communicate, distribute—share—beauty.

In its fullness, practicing creation is also very supportive of the movement away from careless disposable consumerism. If we, eventually, revive many of the crafts and also embrace the concept of *wabi-sabi*, then the idea/ideal of the new, pristine, and machine manufactured need not persist as acceptable or desirable standards of beauty.

A quick note—*wabi-sabi,* a concept we will look at in the honor entropy practice, originated in Japanese culture. It is the acknowledgement of the beauty of transience, imperfection, the impermanent, and the incomplete.

Practicing creation is simple, natural, and fun.

To Practice Creation

1. Practice creating (and being!) solutions. Be causative over your world, not the effect of your environment and circumstances. Don't like your room? Paint! Upset about pollution in the oceans? Join an existing protest organization or start one in your area. If you live near a body of water, go for a walk along its shore and pick up litter. (Heck, no matter where you live, go for a walk and pick up litter!)

2. Make stuff, friends, and waves.

   Whatever your creating urge, splurge: cook, build, plant, sew, or draw. Express yourself. Though a writer and visual artist, I had a sudden urge to learn needlepoint in my early forties. Despite my career in clothing manufacturing, I'd never sewn or been particularly interested in any of the needle arts before this. But I listened to that inner gnowing—saw with my intuition—and to this day doing needlepoint gives me great satisfaction and a certain kind of "peace of the making." Not to mention, I always have some handmade gifts conveniently on hand.

In an altogether different venue of creation, by creating awareness of gender differences in epilepsy with a small group of like-minded people, I helped the neurology research community acknowledge this issue, vastly improving the life of women and girls with epilepsy.

3. It's the process, not the product. We have been trained to focus too much, I feel, on the outcome of our endeavors.

   I want to share a personal epiphany I had about this. While writing this book, I was also doing visual artwork—monoprints, mostly, and some assemblage, which is sort of three-dimensional collage. I was also blogging about True Beauty. One day, a blog-reading acquaintance said to me something like, "Oh, you write about beauty and then go make it in your studio!"

   While it was probably a glib remark, internally I totally recoiled from that statement. My actual thought, when it finally coalesced in my consciousness, was, "Oh no! Do people think *I* think my artwork is True Beauty! Egad! *Oh no!*"

   Of course, another part of me argued about what did I care what others thought? But I did—because I did not want to be unclear or confuse the message about the importance of True Beauty. So here is my truth of it: It is the *process* of making art that is the True Beauty, the act of True Beauty. It is not the piece of art, successful or not in my judgment or others'. It is the process of making—of making anything—that is the method and practice of True Beauty. *Beauty is a verb,* I like to say. *Beauty as action is what makes a difference.*

4. Give of yourself; it is an act of creating relationship and community. It is a beauty-ful act.

Nowhere else is the sacredness of the everyday more evident than in the making. Of food. Of shelter. Of family connections and supports. Of play!

> *When I am working on a problem I never think about beauty. I only think about how to solve the problem. But when I have finished, if the solution is not beautiful, I know it is wrong.*
>
> —Buckminster Fuller

XII. Practice Beauty in Trade and Commerce

Omnia vivunt, omnia inter se conexa.
Everything is alive; everything is interconnected.
—CICERO

HERE IS WHAT the oldest profession *really* is: Trade. Exchange. Commerce.

Call it what you will, but the members of our species have *never* been totally independent of one another. Going way back, we could hypothesize that one gathered, the other hunted—and when they sat down together to eat, they *traded* bites of their collective bounty. We are interdependent.

Creating a useful product that meets an as yet unfulfilled need falls under the aegis of the truly beautiful when it is an elegant solution to a problem, to use the mathematical analogy. (Remember the chapter on creation and how creating is integral to practicing True Beauty and is, in fact, limitless and undefinable.) It is possible, through commerce (sustainable and responsible commerce), to replicate for the many a single beautiful thing or elegant solution. "Beauty brings copies of itself into being. It makes us draw it, take photographs of it, or describe it to other people." (Elaine Scarry, *On Being and Being Just.*)

A Long Story

As told earlier, in the mid-seventies, I thought up a solution to a problem (uncomfortable breast movement while running), turned it into a tangible product (invented the sports bra, then called the "Jogbra"), marketed it, and—to my great surprise—created a multimillion-dollar business around it.

But the dollars were only an indicator of my having hit upon the elegant solution for a need that existed for a significant number of women and girls. It removed a barrier to their participation in athletics! I had just responded to an authentic need of my own and figured out how to make it available to others. The consideration, "If I have this need, I bet a lot of other women runners do too!" was integral here, as was the desire to follow through on it. I then enrolled others in the vision to help manifest it and stuck with it and persevered.

Later, when I found that I'd evolved from struggling artist into a bona fide businessperson, complete with employees, ad budgets, profits, and what the outer world defined as success, I heard myself telling artist friends that "business was the most creative medium I'd ever tried," which while true, did little to quell their astonishment at my metamorphosis. Or mine.

I've given talks, taught business courses, and written articles around entrepreneurship. In the early years of transitioning from writer/craftsperson/painter to businesswoman, one of the things that stood out to me was the similarities between these two pursuits. It is a bit odd, I admit, but to me it felt like my canvas was the industry I was in. And I was literally designing garments, the finished products of which were like the medium being applied on that canvas. In the effort to explain this totally new creation "sports bra," I was writing and directing ad copy and visuals and "teaching" buyers about its value and use. I was creating business systems to keep track of it all, and as it evolved, I kept hiring people who were better at the needed tasks than I ever could have been. It all came together and created a new understanding, an image, an effect—and eventually, a new industry.

All of the above evolved in service to solving a problem. How is that *not* a creative process?

It is in this comparison, this fledgling understanding of the similarities between artist/maker and business builder, that the True Beauty connection between my two pursuits began to dawn. Creation is part of True Beauty; businesses are built by people endeavoring to create solutions to meet needs and solve problems. Hence, if sustainable and responsible, then a commercial endeavor can be of True Beauty. A big "if," I know. Should that be a reason not to try?

Today, early iterations of the Jogbra reside in the American Museum of History at the Smithsonian and in the Metropolitan Museum of Art's costume collection. The invention of the sports bra is considered a revolutionary piece of women's athletic wear and, along with the passing of Title IX in 1972, credited with positively impacting the access to sports and exercise for women and girls everywhere.

So that is the end of the story of how I began to think about True Beauty in relation to commerce, the economic energy of our civilization. But the story goes on. Jogbra was only the beginning. There is the old saying, "When one door closes, another opens."

A Personal Story

As I mentioned before, I learned a great deal in those years and confronted some myths about myself and the world. It was an education on all levels: physical, intellectual, and spiritual. Someday, I'll write *that* book.

Suffice it to say that my priorities were made clearer to me by coming through that adventure. Not least of which was, after selling the Jogbra business, having that existential period of thought about what really, *really* matters.

As a result, I started reading and studying, trying to understand why beauty had come up as what really matters, and I happened upon Elaine Scarry. In her book, *On Beauty and Being Just,* she articulates the relationship between what I am calling the "practice of beauty" and the impulse to create commerce, a (*gasp!*) business: "This phenomenon of {copying beauty} sponsors…the idea of eternity, the perpetual duplicating of a moment that never stops. But *it also sponsors the idea of terrestrial plenitude and distribution, the will to make 'more and more' so that eventually there will be 'enough.'*" (The emphasis is mine.)

This helped me understand that what I had been doing and what I was feeling called to do were not necessarily so disparate. The overriding sense that there was something *other* calling to me was not truly other, it was just the *next* in my personal evolution. Having been an artist before starting the Jogbra business, it felt as if one creation, the business, was finished, and another was waiting to be born.

Though I had discovered business to be a very creative medium, I wondered, all these years and experiences later, who I was now? Did I still know the right end of a paintbrush? Had all those years of writing ad copy and sweating over financial balance sheets corrupted my inner artist?

So I had a hard think through, the existential period referred to earlier, coming up with this odd "beauty!" thing. Confusing "beauty" and "art" (as do most people), I went back into the studio and confronted my creative self. I was calling my own bluff about (still) being an artist. Too many years of wearing a business suit—both literally and figuratively—were making me doubt myself.

I asked myself another question. Directly on the wall of my combination office/studio, using large Magic Markers, I wrote a message to myself:

HOW can I
CREATE
SUPPORT
be
SURROUNDED
by
B E A U T Y ??

That graffiti on my wall was my constant reminder, a directional signal, a constant question that led me back to creating in a different way, outside the world of commerce.

Eventually I was led to formally continue my studies and went on to earn a master's degree.

In those studies, one thing that has become abundantly clear is that our indifference to True Beauty has degraded our culture. From experience, I know that commerce is an effective tool in driving that result. I also believe that the power of commerce can change that outcome.

If we can restructure commerce and reintroduce the importance of True Beauty, we have a chance to turn Western culture around.

The Importance of the Practice

We need to stop looking at commerce and business the way it *has* been done—the too often greedy, wanton, and exploitative ways that have intensified and proliferated. While embracing and including it, this practice attempts to go beyond the notion of "right livelihood" as I understand it. Infusing beauty into our commercial equations is *restructuring* commerce as we go forward, evolving commerce as we ourselves evolve.

Let's contemplate a new era. Thomas Moore plants the seed: "At different times in our history we have denied soul to classes of beings we have wanted to control. Women...slaves... In our day we assume that things do not have soul, and thus we can do to them what we will. A revival of the doctrine of anima mundi would give soul back to the world of nature and artifact." (Moore, *Care of the Soul.*)

Moore further contends (and validates for those of us already suspicious of this) that "made things have a soul." Do we treat them as if? Imagine! A *soul-ecology*, as Moore names it, or *soul consciousness,* might evolve. A consciousness and perception based on appreciation, mindfulness, and respect would encourage and birth truly beautiful patterns of relationship, especially as they relate to those patterns in commerce. (Recall our work in Harmonic Relationships here.)

In today's world, the practice of mindfulness may begin to recognize and honor an ensouled world, but that depends very much upon the practitioner and the depth of awareness, or more likely the willingness to consider *everything* as a sentient being with soul.

My position is that there is no such thing as an inanimate object. Incorporating this kind of consciousness, we can begin to evolve business and commerce into a practice of True Beauty and forever change the way we look at and "do" business.

Before the advent of the Industrial Revolution (late 1700s to mid-1800s), things were made and grown mostly by hand. The tools and machines that were also employed were people or animal powered. A cobbler made shoes: the sole, the upper leathers, the eyelets. A furniture maker carved posts and legs, made joinery. Glass blowers made lamps and bowls and tended the fierce heat of their furnaces. There was an intimate relationship between the maker and the made, creator and created. It was easier to see and feel the soul in the gleaming smooth saddle Mr. Smith made for you.

Because of this, things were fewer and handed down generation to generation. There was a sense of lineage—my great-grandmother's lace tablecloth, silverware, candlesticks, and so on. These were appreciated and used, over and over again. Whatever care and love the maker infused into the object was enhanced by each person who polished, washed, enjoyed, and appreciated using it. There was nothing mystical about it. It was the way things were, just simple common sense.

When machines took over the majority of the making, our attitudes shifted. In many areas, quality suffered to keep prices down. "Things" became disposable. New was good; old was undesirable. Today it is cheaper to buy a new sofa than to reupholster the old one, shocking and unheard of just thirty years ago.

Yet machine-made things have soul also, as do the machines that made them. They are all made of the same matter we are, jostling around in their assigned matter patterns, holding true. They deserve some respect.

Some Thought Experiments

Because this notion flies in the face of so much of what we take for granted and threatens the very heart of our way of consuming, I have a few thought exercises I'd like to invite you to do.

Please do them more than once if you can. But don't try to do them all at once. Do one then come back and do another later. Have some fun with this!

Now, read below and then close your eyes and imagine....

1. Imagine if all new building, all restoration, all creation of *stuff*—garment manufacturing, electronic and technological manufacturing, food production, you name it—was done with a sense of anima mundi, everything having a soul, and was treated as such. How would you change or alter the way you treat things? Would any municipal or governmental systems have to change in response? How about distribution systems for clothing? How might raising food change?

2. Consider: if an architect and a construction company, upon taking on a building project, had to consider the "BQ"—the development's "beauty quotient" as well as the ROI. Or better yet, what if *in* the ROI equation, beauty was a factor along with the dollars and interest earnings calculations (the ROA, or Return on Aesthetics.)? It might read, "Capital investment of twenty million dollars, two years of construction, loss of twelve old-growth trees and one acre of wetlands. ROI: Dollars: *X* percent within five years. Wetlands: one year: a new pond stocked with regional fish; installation of twenty-two new trees with life expectancy of one hundred years; ROI/ROA expected in five/twenty-five years."

3. Think in terms of the True Beauty practices and imagine you are the director of your town's "Office of Beauty Management." (OBM). What's in your job description?

4. How would having an ROA impact an urban landscape? Suburban landscape?

5. Remember that we are in dynamic relationship with all, and it with us. Contemplate the implications of practicing these beauty concepts.

To Practice Beauty and Trade in Commerce

I know this is a tall order. But remember, imagination births vision, and our vision will create our future.

As stated at the beginning of this chapter, the oldest profession is trade. We will always be trading, exchanging with one another, and engaging in commerce. So how do we practice this in a truly beautiful way in the here and now? How to do it with respect for ourselves and in harmony with all the other ensouled entities involved? How, especially in these times when to do so is to go against the prevailing belief and behavioral systems?

To be honest, I do have a difficult time envisioning a soul in Tupperware. But I believe it is there, if only a small soul. I have a less difficult time gnowing it exists in my set of ceramic nesting bowls, made in China. Or my oriental rug. Or my favorite coffee mug. To be aware of anima mundi, to divest oneself of the assumption of an economy based on replaceable disposables, is not only better-best for the ecology but also for your own personal environment and the energy field of the planet. To start at this basic point of recognition and respect will, I believe, have a domino effect on other, more sophisticated ills of commerce—greed, avarice, and fraud. So here are some suggestions on how we might practice True Beauty in commerce these days:

1. First, in your personal business dealings, always be in alignment with your beliefs and values as much as is possible. Endeavor not to trade or deal with those you know to be antithetical to these. I am fond of saying, "Vote with your dollars!"

2. Ditto regarding your professional business dealings. If you are self-employed, this is, of course, far more within your control. To the extent that you control any budgets at work, you can make a difference.

3. Do the research to support points one and two. I know I have been guilty of saying, "But I didn't know!" And, let's face it—sometimes research yields unhappy news, like discovering your favorite chocolate maker is a division of "Giant Evil Corp."

4. Practice looking at made things differently. They are not inanimate; they are a swirling mass of matter in an articulated energy field. Did someone once cherish a piece of furniture in your home? Do you? Respect it; treat it well. Is there a bowl or a pan in the kitchen that you prefer using? Does it give you pleasure to use? Smile back at it the next time you pull it out. Give 'er a kiss! This beauty-practice stuff is not all serious work—in fact, it's often downright playful!

5. When time to dispose of something, do it mindfully. Send it your gratitude for its service.

6. Exchange fairly. If you take care of mechanical things in your home, they will give you years of service. If you

treat your customers well, they will come back. If you treat those who provide a service politely and kindly, they will do their best for you. You get the drift…exchange fairly and kindly.

True Beauty is an applied art and applied philosophy, if you will. To reiterate, beauty is not just a noun, but a *verb.* We need to introduce beauty as a practice into our consciousness to progress and succeed in the "New Story" or the "paradigm shift" or whatever one wants to call this emergent evolution.

We have lived by the assumption that what was good for us would be good for the world. And this has been based on the even flimsier assumption that we could know with any certainty what was good even for us. We have fulfilled the danger of this by making our personal pride and greed the standard of our behavior toward the world - to the incalculable disadvantage of the world and every living thing in it. And now, perhaps very close to too late, our great error has become clear. It is not only our own creativity - our own capacity for life - that is stifled by our arrogant assumption; the creation itself is stifled. We have been wrong. We must change our lives…we must learn to acknowledge that the creation is full of mystery; we will never entirely understand it. We must abandon arrogance and stand in awe…For I do not doubt that it is only on the condition of humility and reverence before the world that our species will be able to remain in it.

—Wendell Berry, The Art of the Commonplace: The Agrarian Essays

XIII. Practice Finding the Funny

Laughter is the best medicine.
—Anonymous

A universal expression of True Beauty is laughter. Laughter needs no translation. We recognize it in any culture, in any demographic.

The quote above I first encountered in a doctor's office. I was a child, bored in the waiting room, and there was a thick, little periodical sitting on the table next to me, *Reader's Digest.* I was interested only in the cartoons scattered throughout. But there was also a section with a short, funny story, purported to be plucked from real life somewhere in vast America, in a section titled "Laughter Is the Best Medicine."

Nowadays we can go online and find that the latest experts are, in fact, researching and touting the health benefits of humor and the act of laughing. Don't we all gnow that? I mean, really, who feels crappy after a good laugh?

There are calories burnt by laughing; blood pressure is positively affected by laughing; a sense of humor can alleviate stress. It is all there measured, quantified, hypothesized, and ratified by various doctors, PhDs, and such.

All we need to gnow and know here is that engaging in and with humor helps to create balance in our environment, to restore harmony. Laughter is the music of True Beauty, becoming.

Humor is everywhere, really. We just have to be on the lookout for it, *see* it! It is the paradoxical and ironical interactions between us, in our environment. It is when intention and the counterintention come together in a most silly way. Slapstick comedy is a physical illustration of this. Paradox is the cosmos itself having a laugh.

Looking for humor in a situation is an avenue of perception, a *way* of perceiving. It might be as mundane as a seagull strutting its stuff up and down the pier that strikes one as funny or as macabre as the story below. Unless practicing straight-up *Seeing* (the first beauty practice), we are usually looking at the world through a lens (or three or five).

It may be a critical lens. You've met that person—always finding what's wrong in every situation. It may be a safety lens, always scanning for danger spots and safe zones. Or it may be the mother lens. You know, the "eyes in the back of her head" ability. Just as these exist, so does the lens of humor.

Humor can be physical, visual, and auditory. It is slapstick for one, parody for some, double entendres, or nonsense words for still others. Humor is in the eye of the beholder as much as beauty. Or should I say, humor is in the belly of the laugher?

But it is cultivating and holding the desire and ability to see "the funny" in your interactions, circumstances, and environment that is the magic, the True Beauty. Choosing to employ this lens of humor through which you sense and perceive the world becomes a gift not only for yourself but to others as well.

A Story

While finding the funny could be as simple as seeing that seagull strut and having a quiet chuckle with yourself, it also might be as unusual and quirky as the time my sister, Victoria, and I could not stop breaking into peals of laughter while making a death mask of my mother's recently embalmed face.

Victoria, an artist and art therapist, had been making cast masks of various friends and family members in that era of her artist evolution. Although Mother and she had talked about it, V had been unable to cast a mask of her face before Mother became terminally ill.

So it happened that one evening, shortly after Mother died, we were sitting together in the kitchen of our parents' home, talking as siblings do. Victoria mourned the lost opportunity of capturing Mom's face—the aquiline nose, deep-eye sockets, those "rosebud" lips, as she had called them. Her body was scheduled for the crematorium the next afternoon.

"Why not do it now?" I asked boldly, only sort of rhetorically.

Victoria replied, "Nah. Wouldn't work. You need the body's heat to dry the cast...."

"Isn't there Vaseline on the face so it slips off?" I asked. I'd had the experience myself at V's hands, so I fancied myself experienced.

"Not enough," she replied. "Need heat. Or it might just harden right on there and not come off. I dunno, really."

"Oh, so...no other way?"

"Hmmm..."

"...hair dryer maybe?"

"Only heats up the outside. Though...still, it might work."

"If it didn't...?"

"Like I said, might stick to her face..." We both took a silent moment to contemplate a hard, white mask not coming off Mother's face.

Victoria's voice dropped to a whisper, "Or maybe her skin would come up with the mask?" We looked at each other in horror. And then started laughing. Nervous, frightened laughter.

"Mother would hoot!" Mother would have loved the idea, the risk, the adventure. But she would not have liked any public indignities.

"You could *never* tell anyone!" Victoria gasped at me. She meant our brothers. She meant if something went horribly awry.

"Of course not!" I gasped back.

Somewhere in there, we had made the decision. We would try to capture our mother's face for posterity. If it didn't work, she would go to the fires like the undercover rebel she had always been in life. And it would be our secret.

In the silent, stuffy, and shadowy funeral parlor, my sister and I looked down on the still contours and planes of a face that had once danced with my mother's spirit. The rosebud lips were bright with her "Love That Pink" lipstick. The awful blue eye shadow she insisted on wearing lay on the broad, expansive eyelids I had always admired. The funeral parlor people had done a bang-up job with the makeup.

"Why did they do the whole embalming and makeup thing if she's going into the furnace this afternoon?" I asked V, gazing at the strange face below me.

"I dunno. Viewing, probably. It'll make our job easier, I think. When I do the mask, if the makeup comes up with it, it could make the cast really cool!" We sort of looked at one another with big eyes—were we ghouls? Then we laughed.

It was a bit touchy gaining permission from the funeral parlor guy to go mess with his handiwork. We decided to adopt the "it's-our-mother-of-course-we-can-do-this" attitude. Remember, this was many years back before the concept of death masks was on the radar screen of the mainstream funeral industry in North America.

So with a bravado that masked our nerves, Victoria began with me as her helper. With a stainless-steel bowl of water and white strips of plaster-of-paris-coated gauze, V began laying the damp strips I handed her across our mother's still face.

"Looks kinda like a mummy."

"No pun intended, I hope." Roll of eyes in response.

"Well," Victoria said, "at least I don't have to worry about leaving nostril holes for breathing!"

"God, Vic! You're *so* sensitive!"

"No! Really! It was one of the things that stopped her from agreeing to do this before she got sick. She couldn't stand the idea of straws sticking out of her nose to breathe through while the mask dried! Now it's not a problem!"

We looked at each other, down at Mother's partially bandaged face, and imagined brightly colored drinking straws sticking out of that elegant nose. Of course she wouldn't do that.

The quiet got on my nerves, and I began singing quietly.

"Are you humming 'Whistle While You Work'?!" V looked up briefly in disbelief. "From the old Snow White?"

I stopped for a moment and realized she was right. We cracked up, then started singing and humming together. Between giggles and song, we applied more Vaseline and continued layering the casting strips that looked like bandages onto my mother's face. We imagined the disapproving and scandalized mortician lurking somewhere in the back as we worked our women's magic on our mother's remains.

The obnoxious sound of our hair dryer in that quiet place startled us and made us laugh anew. I could feel Mother's presence, just *see* that mischievous smile on her face as she stepped over some line or took some liberty, flashing her blue eyes at me, her tiny accomplice.

Today the successful result of that long-ago afternoon's work hangs on a wall in my sister's house. Indeed, Mother's too-blue eye shadow and a bit of mascara call attention to those deep-set eyelids. And I am reminded, again, of the importance of humor in this both/and universe in which we all live—and die.

The Importance of the Practice

Have you noticed, it is the *presence of the spirit* of humor that can make all the difference in how a situation is perceived? How many times have you said, "Well, you had to be there," when retelling what was, for you, a hilarious episode, yet did not elicit a laugh from your listener? Like the examples above, they pale in the retelling. The funny factor seems to evaporate without some inner alchemy recalling it into the retelling.

It is our sensing of the field of paradox that tickles our funny bones—our spirit of fun. We smile, we feel mischievous, and we laugh. In the presence of the spirit of humor, in its field, we are in delight! When we hear of it, when it is retold, it is still powerful and we can still laugh, but I would encourage those researchers on the web to take a look at the health benefits. I bet they are not quite as rich.

And this is why it is important to cultivate a sense of humor and practice it. It is just not enough to hear of it or experience it secondhand. It is magical to be in it, be it. To laugh out loud.

When was the last time you wet your pants laughing?

Humor is one of the greatest teachers. Its withdrawal from and repression within academia is a contributor to our educational system's lackluster reputation and performance statistics—one of the benchmarks of our cultural decline.

We cannot end a discussion of the importance of humor without also discussing its dark side. The power of humor is evident, as is the negativity of its power when wielded through sarcasm, derision, and ridicule. There is definitely a place for parody. British comedy has proven that "making fun of" has a sharp and clever role in showing ourselves to ourselves. But sarcasm is the lowest form of humor and the most common and popular form in declining civilizations. Derision and snarky ridicule serve only to polarize and separate, underscoring hostilities. They have no place in the Practice of True Beauty.

To Practice Cultivating, Nurturing, and Exercising Your Sense of Humor

1. Read the comics in the newspaper or whatever light reading appeals to you. Being grown up doesn't exclude "the funnies."

2. Notice the paradoxical and ironic connections that life serves up. Comment on them to friends. It may end up in a comic riff that produces good belly laughs all around! By sharing something you find funny, you project the spirit of humor onto those around you, which will likely result in a harmonious connection.

3. Let something unexpected dissolve into a humorous event rather than an inconvenient or offensive one.

4. Choose companions who appreciate and share your brand of humor.

5. Endeavor to laugh out loud once a day.

6. Humor is a personal taste; have fun, go practice, and enjoy your own brand. Laugh out loud at least once a day!

Laughter resides in the heart chakra; let there be light.

Odd fact: A good belly laugh is beneficial for the lymphatic system.

XIV. Practice Taking Sanctuary

It is in deep solitude that I find the gentleness with which I can truly love my brothers. The more solitary I am the more affection I have for them...Solitude and silence teach me to love my brothers for what they are, not for what they say.

—Thomas Merton

The practice of seeking and keeping a sanctuary is important to the sustainability of the Way of Beauty. To sustain and nurture a cohesive beauty awareness, to be a "cultural creative" and an agent for change in our turbulent times, it is very helpful to have a safe haven; I might even say it is imperative. Everyone needs his or her own safe haven from the busyness.

A conscious practitioner of beauty must have a place to refresh, be nourished, and even, sometimes, be appreciated. I am speaking here of an explicitly physical place. One's sanctuary is a material manifestation of the beauty state of mind. Sanctuary is a place to be still, a place where one's expectation of the experience of harmony is the norm, a place of serenity in which one might also create. It is a place of safety. To wit, a place unchallenged.

Of course, we *may* go to our sanctuaries to jump around and dance and shout. These are our sanctuaries—where we can express however we need/want, from silence, meditation, and serenity to drumming, dancing, or shouting; a Sufi may twirl!

Like all else, our sanctuaries can evolve. The reality is that all physical places are prone to dissolution. Transition is a necessary part of transformation.

A Story

I am reminded of the Russian family I stayed with while in the country teaching entrepreneurship to an organization of Russian women. This family of four lived in a fifth-floor, government-owned apartment in the city of Petrozavodsk in northern Russia. The elevator in the building hadn't worked in years, they told me as we trudged up the concrete stairway with my suitcase. And they would know since they had lived in the same apartment for twenty-five years.

The family had, quite literally, grown and grown up in their little five-room apartment they were generously sharing with me for two weeks. The children were now young adults who were happy to try their English on me and I my Russian on them.

I was impressed at how efficiently they used their space. It was very homey, and there was a place for everything—keys and coats on the wall as you came in the door; shoes off as well. There were many shelves for books and dishes. The tiny kitchen had a large window, the sill of which held a window box brimming with a profusion of herbs and a bright-red geranium.

I marveled at how they sorted out themselves and their things—schoolbooks, groceries, sundry packages—at the end of each day. There were nooks and crannies for all. But it didn't take long for me to understand that the father had temporarily moved out so that I might be their guest.

One day, toward the end of my stay, they had what appeared to be a family conference. At its end, they turned to me and the daughter, Tamara, said in her quite good English, "We have something to show you. Come!" We all bundled into their small car, Tamara sitting on her brother's lap. I had no idea where we were going.

The father drove us out of the city. We passed pastures and fields. Having been confined to government meeting halls and offices in the city during my visit, I hadn't seen any of this. We turned off onto a bumpy dirt road passing rustic little wooden cottages every so often, sitting in what appeared to be overgrown and weedy yards. Some, I noticed, had cultivated vegetable gardens plotted neatly right in the midst of overgrown yards. I thought I spotted some berry bushes too.

I started looking more carefully at some of the smaller trees, wondering if they might be fruit trees. What fruits grew in northern Russia, I wondered. Then, suddenly, we turned into the drive of one of these cottages.

With whoops of glee, the family piled out of the car and surged toward their little house. "Our dacha!" Tamara turned to me and said with a very broad smile on her face. "Our sanctuary in the country!"

And suddenly I knew how they "fit" into their tiny city apartment. They didn't. They had, both physically, psychically, and spiritually their sanctuary in the country.

The Importance of the Practice

The point of creating sanctuary is to create an *intentionally nurturing* retreat that is readily at hand. It may be your home or a room in your home. Or a studio. It can be a garden or even a portion of a garden. It can be all these things, as one doesn't have to be limited to one sanctuary place. What it must be is this: pleasing to its occupant.

Virginia Woolf articulated this concept among modern women with her declaration that one must have "a room of one's own." In articulating what facilitates the presence of True Beauty in our lives, I underscore the sanctity aspect of that "room," that it must have the quality of being safe and beautiful—a place where the entire field of potentialities is able to open up to you.

Creating a sanctuary doesn't need to be complicated. It can be as simple or as elaborate as you choose. It can be about an activity that calms you (as Virginia Woolf wrote) or just a meditation pillow in a corner.

I actually have several sorts of sanctuaries. My art studio space is a sanctuary for me. The act of *making* itself is sacred for me and puts me in a harmonic flow. I do not hold classes there or entertain there; I am clear it is my sacred space. I've also set aside a corner of the studio with a plump little loveseat, footstool, table, and lamp. Here I read, meditate, or just sit in stillness.

There is one sanctuary I travel to, several states away. It is a geographical landscape with which I resonate deeply, and I am blessed to have a dear friend living there with whom I stay one month each year. It is rather far out in "the boonies." There is no television, dishwasher, or microwave. I sit on the porch and listen to birds, watch the rain, follow the cloud shadows as they cross the water and the mountains beyond.

Sanctuary implies a state of not being able to be harmed. A safe state. To be "in sanctuary" is to leave anxiety and worry at the doorstep.

Sanctuary is often our home, no matter how consciously we practice and nurture this fact. And sometimes we find sanctuary that is not a physical place, but a person. Sometimes we are fortunate enough and there are members of our family who also serve as a sanctuary. You know the ones: the spouse, sibling, or cousin who feels like a kindred spirit. Even when you argue, you know the foundation springs from caring. In this respect, we see again how one True Beauty practice supports and influences another, as the Practice of Taking Sanctuary has ties into the Practice of Harmonic Relationships.

When there is a safe place, full of supportive and known (not perfect!) people we consider family, we are truly blessed with a key beauty component. But this takes work. And place, a sacred place—sanctuary—is a part of that work.

To Create Your Sanctuary and Practice Using It

1. Look around you. Is there a place in your life already serving as your sanctuary, but you haven't named it as such? If so, recognize this, and use it with greater mindfulness. Put up artwork or fresh flowers; intentionally add beauty—whatever that means to you.

2. If you're starting fresh, think about where you like to sit (or walk) and relax. Identify the quiet times and places available to you in your world. Use your other True Beauty practices: Think with your heart and see it as well in your mind's eye. Name it to yourself "Sanctuary."

3. Go to your sanctuary regularly. Can you do so once a day? If it is home or within your home, this will make it easier. Go "into retreat" regularly, a mind-set as well as a location. Here are some possible ways:
    a. Go home for lunch!
    b. Go sit outside.
    c. Take an opportunity to sit quietly between one project or task and another. Observe small things. Listen.
    d. Meditate if you like.
    e. Do all of the above, simultaneously.

4. Allow what "sanctuary" means to you to blossom and change with you over time. This is your time, your place. Time for you, with you. It is in sanctuary that beauty most readily seeps into us, from us. Sometimes it may include others, sometimes not.

5. Consider the people in your life. Do any have the potential to be, or are already, a kindred spirit—a sanctuary in relationship?

So, get moving, have fun, and use the K.I.S.S.method in creating your sanctuary!

> *I love my family, my children...but inside myself is a place where I live all alone and that's where you renew your springs that never dry up.*
>
> —Pearl S. Buck

XV. Practice the Pursuit of Happiness

The happiness that is genuinely satisfying is accompanied by the fullest exercise of our faculties and the fullest realization of the world in which we live.

—BERTRAND RUSSELL

DO YOU SEE the glass as half full or half empty?

"Pursuit of happiness"—it's in America's Declaration of Independence, and it is an integral part of practicing beauty. Integrating beauty is about broadening harmony, and creating harmony has a great deal to do with each individual's ability to understand his or her own experience of happiness. And that is something that has become increasingly elusive in our modern society.

So, what's the trick?

See the proverbial glass. The *whole* damn glass. See it half full *and* half empty. Remember the Both/And Practice? Cultivating happiness and the ability to have happiness is about choice and our continuum of choices. But at its root, being happy is being able to *see*, to observe the whole glass and *still* choose to emphasize its fullness. So we have come, quite beautifully, full circle: back to the ability to *see*, our first practice in order to have happiness, almost our last primary practice.

In their book, *How We Choose to Be Happy*, Rick Foster and Greg Hicks did an impressive survey of how people achieve and maintain happiness. They were not looking for the "rose-colored glasses" kind of happiness, either, but rather those who felt all emotions deeply. Their survey revealed that consistently happy people were far from being in denial about the less than optimal, shall we say, aspects of their lives. The paradox is that to experience great happiness, we must sometimes also be able to experience life's greatest sorrows. Their work proposes that happiness is, perhaps, a long-term emotional state that can carry us through all that dishes up.

In fact, it is from the Foster/Hicks survey that the proverbial water-glass metaphor is resurrected. One of its foremost results was the uncovering this ability by those deemed to maintain sustainable happiness to see the glass as *both* half full *and* half empty; that is, to see the balance in each situation, pros and cons, good and bad, and then to *choose* to concentrate on the positive. This, according to the authors, creates stable happiness.

Seeing the whole glass is a True Beauty ability. Being aware of the complexities, of the polarities necessary to create balance, bequeaths a sense of harmony. To see only a part is to experience only a fragment. Having only that experience, one tends to reflect only a segment—to be one-sided or fragmented.

Seeing the glass, whatever it holds and how much of each, is to allow for the both/and universe. It allows for all the layers of truth. It gives space for our authentic self to be still, perhaps take a moment…and to choose to see the good in the situation.

Choose happiness.

To Practice Pursuing and Increasing the Catch of Happiness

1. Make sure you are being honest with yourself about yourself. (Practice Authenticity!)

2. Take responsibility for your own circumstances: you are in charge of your situation and your attitude!

3. Make a list of what specific feelings you associate with being happy. Review it once a year.

4. Identify those things, people, and events, both small and big, that contribute to your feelings of contentedness. There may be similarities with the list you created for the Harmonic Relationships Practice. Refer to it.

5. Again, surround yourself with higher companions, those who have your best interests at heart. Politely avoid those in "naysayer mode."

6. If you fall into a dark place for a bit, recognize it, don't bury it. Take it out for a walk. Own it. Once you've had a good cry or rant, open your eyes and your heart and have a look around. Look farther and see what's next. While it is often advisable to seek help from friends during difficult times, do not fly your anguish like a flag for all to see. We are all so much more than our wounds and so vulnerable when the wounds are fresh.

7. When called for, do "the two-minute drill." Put your mouth into a smile for two minutes straight, without a break. You'll be surprised how your mood can shift and follow your mouth!

   This "drill" became a routine when I was struggling with my own habit of being negative too often, too quickly. I was living with someone who had the same predilection, and pretty unconsciously for a time, we were reinforcing this habit in one another. Needless to say, it did not produce contentment.

   Think about it: when you are busy finding fault, isn't your face (inner if not outer face) all scrunched up in a frown? So, to dispel this inner critic, this grouchy old lady who lived in me, I decided to smile her away.

   But I knew that my partner had to do it too. So, the two-minute drill was born. Whenever we started grousing to each other—even about some small thing—one of us would hold up a hand and say "Uh! Two-minute drill time!" and we would both turn up the corners of our respective mouths.

   It worked every time. The critic evaporated, and a true smile—sometimes laughter—came instead.

   You don't have to have a partner to institute the two-minute drill. It's just how it happened for me. It works just fine solo.

8. Always remember: This too shall pass. So cherish the light and respect and endure the darkness.

Happiness is a particularly enhanced, perhaps human, state of harmony. It is an important beauty practice. Do not think for a moment it is trivial or shallow. Some of the happiest people are the most productive.

Because it is an expression of True Beauty, it is no wonder that the Dalai Lama has had a great deal to say about it:

> "The basic thing is that everyone wants happiness, no one wants suffering. And happiness mainly comes from our own attitude, rather than from external factors. If your own mental attitude is correct, even if you remain in a hostile atmosphere, you feel happy….
>
> When we feel love and kindness toward others, it not only makes others feel loved and cared for, but it helps us also to develop inner happiness and peace."

But what is happiness except the simple harmony between a man and the life he leads?

—Albert Camus

XVI. Honoring Entropy

Oh, this is the joy of the rose:
That it blows,
And goes!
—Willa Cather

It seems easier to find beauty in the cycles of coming *into* existence, in growth, and in discovery than on the other side of the creation cycle—decay, dissolution, and imperfection. But what we think of as "destruction" is as vital to creation as "construction," and so honoring entropy is an integral part of the True Beauty cycle and its practice.

If we honor entropy rather than resist it, if we befriend it rather than demonize it, we take a long step away from our engrained fear of the destruction/decay side of a cycle toward serenity, toward harmony and The Way of True Beauty, in the here and the now. This create/destroy relationship is yet another illustration of our both/and universe, is it not?

I want to be clear here. I am using *create* to mean the tendency toward ordering mass/matter into a particular design and/or function. Entropy is the tendency toward order's disintegration into chaos. In scientific terms, it is the slowing down of and eventual inert energy. The word *"destroy*, while the antonym of *create*, implies a more active action than entropy, which in the Beauty Practice I am seeing as a *process*, not necessarily a specific *action*. To illustrate: a sandcastle by the sea is destroyed when someone kicks it down; it suffers entropy as the tide slowly comes in and the waves lap at it, melting it away over time.

Perhaps there is no better way to introduce the idea of honoring entropy as a practice of beauty than to talk about the *wabi-sabi* aesthetic concept.

Evolving from the ancient Japanese Tea Ceremony traditions and still thriving in today's world, *wabi-sabi* is a decidedly non-Western and nonpop-culture method of perceiving beauty. If we are on an automatic pilot way of seeing, we might even perceive a *wabi-sabi* object as ugly or something to be discarded, for "wabi-sabi is a beauty of things imperfect, impermanent, and incomplete." (Koren, *Wabi-Sabi for Artists, Designers, Poets, and Philosophers.*)

A Little Story

> Sen no Rikyu desired to learn The Way of Tea. He visited the Tea Master, Takeno Joo. Joo ordered Rikyu to tend the garden. Eagerly Rikyu set to work. He raked the garden until the ground was in perfect order. When he had finished he surveyed his work. He then shook the cherry tree, causing a few flowers to fall at random onto the ground. The Tea Master Joo admitted Rikyu to his school. http://www.soika.com/links/text/03e_wabisabi.htm.)

Wise Rikyu revealed the beauty of the transient cherry blossoms.

What happened there? The potential student, Rikyu, illustrated his awareness of the beauty of the transient, dying, fallen flowers against the perfectly arranged ground. He showed an awareness of the beauty of their ephemeral nature. The Japanese honor and codify this knowingness with their celebration of *wabi-sabi.*

This centuries-old concept is an aesthetic of the transient, imperfect, and austere; it is an affirmation of the beauty felt in melancholy. Haven't we all felt, sometimes, the beauty surrounding a sadness? A flower fading or a sun setting; the beautiful blazing autumnal colors of New England are its dying leaves. Honoring entropy acknowledges and embraces the changes that come with aging and all the cycles of that change.

The word *patina* is often found in descriptions and definitions of *wabi-sabi.* I believe this is because age and experience applies layers to any face: the beauty of peeling paint on the face of a long-used boat, the deep green-black of old copper, or the gray of salt-soaked driftwood. *Wabi-sabi* is the beauty of the withered, the weathered, and the scarred. Further, it insinuates simplicity and quietude. There is a note of nostalgia to it.

This validates and celebrates entropy as an attractive and pleasing point in what we might name the "beauty continuum."

The Importance of the Practice

It is this connected continuum that I want to focus on here for a moment and put forward the proposition that there really is *no* stable point of perfection—or anything else. Think of this in relation to the concepts of the beautiful and the ugly. Of entropy and birth.

What if that which is commonly perceived as ugliness is only a transition period between points of the beautiful? The out-of-whackness is on the way to becoming—*in whack*? In harmony? To becoming beauty. If we concur that balanced turbulence is part of the orderliness of the universe, that polarities are only complements, that every yin has its dot of yang, and vice versa, then beauty must have its complement, its balance. And with this complement, this "other," how much easier to know it, feel it?

On a daily and mundane level, much beauty is commonly perceived—mistaken—as ugly or not beauty. This often happens when we are in our shortcut method of perceiving and sensing, when, on automatic pilot, we in fact do not *see*.

A glowing-red traffic light on a dark, misty night can be beautiful…or perceived as an ugly example of man's mechanistic and unheeding development. But most likely, the traffic light was not *seen* at all; the body as automaton simply steps on the car brake. The red light was never truly *seen*.

A rusting, old tractor in the middle of a fallow field—is it an eyesore, or is it beautiful? Is an animal's rotting carcass repulsive garbage or beautiful compost?

I find it unique and refreshing that *wabi-sabi* embraces the man-made as readily as the natural world. This is an important aspect of this concept of beauty. It blurs the distinction as well as any temptation toward evaluation regarding natural beauty, man-made art versus "art" in nature.

If "rustic" and "elegant" were to marry, they would produce a *wabi-sabi* baby!

In our lives, we cycle through various versions and degrees of entropy many times before the final deaths of our bodies.

When a truth rusts, a companion betrays, or your sanctuary crumbles—it is time to dig into your well of courage and recognize that the cycle is evolving.

Our spirits and personalities grow and stretch and also wither and shrink. We succeed; we fail. Sometimes we just coast.

The martial arts teach us that to not be broken, we must bend. There is cacophony that amazingly returns to harmony. Our bodies begin to decompose. Some believe this happens to each individual human only once; others believe it happens repeatedly. There is no doubt that entropy is also a gateway to true ugliness, and honoring entropy does not mean that the ugly does not exist.

It should be apparent by now that I would not categorize death as un-beautiful. The process of decay and death itself has its own place in the beauty continuum. That part of the cycle holds its own vibration of beauty, and I am grateful that Japanese culture has codified it as *wabi-sabi*. Death is a necessary—and fecund—part of the natural cycle of creation, the process of beauty's making.

It is, however, my position that wanton, *needless* killing of any living thing is ugly. Stupid. Not beautiful. It is a discordant feeling, or as a pop-culture idiom states, "a disturbance in the Force, Obi-Wan."

Common sense (a beautiful thing) and our intuition (our gnowingness) tell us this is so. We react with revulsion to that which is not beautiful, or antisurvival, a threat to our own ability to be ongoing. We feel repulsion.

Conversely, we are attracted to that which is a proponent of our own survival, to that with which we are in step—in fact, to that with which we are in harmonious relationship.

Whether you believe in reincarnation or salvation, the real struggle is to do all of this messy part of living with grace, to honor entropy, and find the *wabi-sabi* elements in the transitional tableau of degradation, impermanence, change, uncertainty, and the eventual emergence of what will be.

Joseph Campbell, a great voice for the mythic in humankind, reminds us repeatedly in his various lectures that our Judeo-Christian culture is one of the few that has separated itself so thoroughly from nature's beauty, from its wisdom. We would do well, as we go forward, to take a page (or twenty) from the ancient tea masters of Japan, as well as the Diné of North America.

When a truth rusts, a companion betrays, or your sanctuary crumbles—it is time to dig into your well of courage and recognize that the cycle is evolving. Call it winter, transition, shadow, or death—whatever resonates with you. It is a necessary part of the only constant: change. We evolve.

Our modern culture has tried to bury this inevitability in elaborate layers of illusion. As chaos theory teaches, it is not chaos that falls from some mysteriously previous order but order that spews forth from the primeval chaos. The isness gloriously and unashamedly starts with a messy, unorganized clamor.

To Practice Honoring Entropy

1. Expect it. Since the cycle of birth/death/rebirth is inherent in all living systems, don't pretend it will not be an integral part of your own experiences. Plan for it, even.

   I am not just talking about the usual run-of-the-mill sort of planning like writing a will and so on. Remember the old saying, "This too shall pass"? We usually invoke it about an unhappy event. But it is also a good thing to remember during the happy times. Planning for the end of a cycle means remaining conscious that even the good, sweet, happy times shall pass. We can only hope *those* passings will be more of an intermission!

2. So practice remembering "this too shall pass." It can be an effective guard against taking those happy events for granted, the difficult ones too hard. There will always be a cycle; it will always include entropy.

3. Practice honing your abilities to be responsive and flexible in the face of those changes requiring dissolution of some sort. Think of job loss and divorce. Both involve major dissolutions of relationships, as well as perhaps status and economics. One's sense of independence and ability to care for oneself are the abilities to keep honed.
    a. Embrace and practice your gnowingness. Stay in touch with your authenticity. Find the funny. In short, review and use of the True Beauty practices to gently assist yourself through the end of a cycle is helpful compassion for yourself.

4. Practice disillusionment! We choose to hold onto a few nice, fuzzy illusions in our modern culture. If we disabuse ourselves of a few, it would help a great deal with the first two practices listed here. So I suggest a conscious attempt at breaking some of these more pervasive cultural illusions and their subsequent behaviors. Do you recognize any of these in yourself?

a. "I am immortal"—not taking care of the body and treating this life as though it has no natural ending point
b. "Nothing's gonna change; I'll do it tomorrow"—procrastination, assuming the opportunity will still be there
c. "Nobody is/everybody is the same as me"—both are true; both aren't true, yes? Yet when viewed as absolutes, as is often the case when we are on automatic pilot, neither allows for cyclical changes. When we acknowledge entropy as a natural part of all processes, we naturally avoid assumptions of stasis.

5. Think compost, not mere garbage. If it is your life circumstances that are decaying and beginning to stink, look for ways the situation might be fodder for the future. If everything is collapsing, is it time to build anew—or plant trees in the new fertilizer?

   We are attracted to those forces, things, people, and events that uplift our spirits, smooth our ways, use our talents, and add to our understanding. But we cannot allow our thinking and perceptions to fall into autopilot on the nature of decay, death, and ugliness any more than we can about birth, life, and beauty.

   Learning to truly appreciate the full cycle by coming to appreciate and honor entropy is part of The Way of True Beauty.

The pain passes, but the beauty remains.

—Pierre Auguste Renoir

The Supporting Practices

THERE ARE CERTAIN practices that have been in the culture for a very long time. Indeed, they have endured through many civilizations and cultures because of their efficacious effect on the human body, mind, and spirit. These are the "Supporting Practices" of the Way of Beauty. They support, enhance, and facilitate each practice, separately and as a whole.

I bet you know them:

Practice the Golden Rule

> *If you contemplate the Golden Rule, it turns out to be an injunction to live by grace rather than by what you think other people deserve.*
>
> — DEEPAK CHOPRA, THE THIRD JESUS: THE CHRIST WE CANNOT IGNORE

It is a core bit of beauty practice: "Do unto others as you would have them do unto you." Neatly incorporating authenticity, compassion, and simplicity in one elegant concept, one might say such practical eloquence needs little editorializing. Things become trite because they are experienced as truth, resonating with many. The Golden Rule is one of these bits of wisdom.

One could argue, however, that this bit of spiritual guidance presupposes a pervasive and uniform morality of "the group." Is it arrogance and dominator-culture thinking to believe that what I want "done unto me" is what another would also desire?

While there is that danger, especially in this age of instant communication that results in the spillover of one culture's mores into another, I still believe we can reclaim the Golden Rule for the greater good and the highest purpose. For on the larger plane, when thinking in terms of karmic law, at least as I understand it, I believe the old Golden Rule still stands up to scrutiny; it still holds true.

To practice beauty as it manifests in the Golden Rule:

1. Feeling compassion, treat others as you would want them to treat you if the situation were reversed.

2. Practice doing this with all species and objects as well, with the idea of anima mundi in mind.

3. Try thinking with the universal declaration of human rights (see Notes section) in mind. Does this affect any perspectives you've been holding?

In treating others as we ourselves would choose to be treated, we are acknowledging our similarities as beings. This is a foundational block of tthe Way of Beauty.

Be Still

If courageous enough, we might just
slow to the pace of creation,
where the pulse by which the mind thinks
touches the pulse by which the heart feels,
and together they equal the rhythm of miracle,
where being plays in exact motion
with all being.

—Mark Nepo

Sit and watch the sky. Or the desert. Or a body of water. Meditate twice a day. Listen to birds at the feeder.

Thomas Moore refers to the "sacred arts of life" and recommends pausing, taking time, and reverie. Ah, the lost art of simple reverie! In our scheduled, formatted, and widely investigated world, we all know about, and may even have, our discipline of meditation…but how many of us *allow* ourselves the sweet, quiet joy of reverie?

Here, I reiterate what many, many before have touted as meaningful spiritual and healing practice: slow down, be still, be *mindful.*

Be Active

> *Healing is closely aligned with beauty. To restore our psyche and soul from the effects of exhaustion, stress and pain, we would do well to enter consciously into the splendor of the physical world. A walk through the fields, a hike to the mountains, a swim in the lake…are salutary for the soul.*
>
> —James Conlon, *The Sacred Impulse*

Whole libraries have been written about the benefits of physical fitness. I don't need to repeat them here; it's all mostly true. Is it Calvinism that calls the body the "temple of the soul"? Our bodies are our vehicle and our suits of flesh. They can fit comfortably or not. If not, they distract and create discord.

Bodies are both messengers and feedback loops as with any living system. To use the body is to avoid early or unnecessary entropy. Like any interrelated system, it will be healthier and feel and work better if used, cared for, and paid attention to.

I can attest to the power of physical exercise in the integration of the mind, body, and spirit and especially in relation to the healing of the spirit and the stimulation of creative energies. Upon becoming a recreational, noncompetitive runner in the 1970s, running about thirty miles a week, it came as a complete and wholly pleasant surprise to me to experience these "side effects" of daily physical exercise.

This was my experience: an active body facilitated the experience of natural beauty, promoted inner serenity, and supercharged my creativity. Such an elegant, healing simplicity!

The human body is a beautiful, intricate, somewhat bizarre, and baroque system. Be beauty in action: *use* it.

The Three Keys of the Way of Beauty

Three being such a magic number, and in honor of the K.I.S.S. Practice, I couldn't resist the temptation to look and see if there were three major actions in the Way of Beauty practices. Were there, perhaps, three essential practices? And once the eye adjusted, sure enough, there they were. If one can do nothing else, these three lead the heart and soul toward True Beauty: Compassion, Relationship, and Creation. In all their various, intense, and messy forms!

The number three has significance in almost every wisdom tradition:

- Virgin. Mother. Crone.
- Father. Son. Holy Ghost.
- Janna. Bhakti. Karma.

These have been the three legs upon which wisdom traditions have stood for long periods.

As a three-legged stool cannot have one leg longer or shorter than another or it will fall over, so it is with wisdom. When one wisdom concept is heralded above all others as superior, "the one," the tradition will eventually become aberrated. The great stool of wisdom will fall over into dark times.

Yet over and over, we try by attempting to comprehend through simplification, by privileging one concept over another and tagging it as "the one" as a way into all wisdom. This is not necessarily untrue or unworkable as a way *in*; it just doesn't work over the long haul or when the wisdom tenets or faith is favored over all others. Whichever concept has been privileged gets lost in dogma and ritual. It stops being *a* truth and becomes *the* truth, and in so being, isn't. I don't need to list all the wars that have been fought with each side claiming religious righteousness on *their* side.

In Christianity, the privileged concept became love. In Eastern philosophies, it appears to be enlightenment that has been privileged, and in our current, very secular-oriented age of reason, we have privileged the "show me" version of scientific knowledge above all else.

Now, rather dangerously, I propose it is the time of beauty, True Beauty. It gave me pause to propose raising another concept into this "privileged" stratum. But (of course) I have my reasons.

Plato, Whitehead, May, Rumi, O'Donohue, Gibran, and many others have, at different points in their ruminations, referenced beauty as source to and of love, spiritual awareness, truth, and consciousness. Beauty is also the outcome or descriptor of harmony, a chicken-and-egg problem here.

Beauty seems very much at the root of a great deal. Is it the source of all?

I had to ask myself: Is beauty in fact the *seat* of the metaphoric wisdom stool—that which all else is endeavoring to uphold, illuminate, and stabilize? Are reason, goodness, and consciousness its legs? Is this possibility reason enough to "give it a go," as this coming era's privileged concept?

Is beauty, perhaps, the source from which all else flows—dark energy, luminous energy, amazing universe? *This* is where the journey of exploring the landscape of beauty, True Beauty, has brought me.

So, I have herein envisioned this concept of beauty as action, placing True Beauty above all other notions as *the* suitable new operating paradigm. I have endeavored to show that it is possible to consciously practice beauty to achieve greater periods of harmony between our inner and outer selves, between humankind, our environment, our fellow species, and of the Many and the One. By so doing, we are also, I believe, actively evolving our consciousness.

So I propose that we each take action, and practice True Beauty. Let's get on that boat named "Paradigm Shift." It's sailing!

A Mission Statement to Reclaim True Beauty

It is the mission of Beauty As Action and The Way of Beauty to reclaim beauty and raise awareness of its higher, true nature; to use this concept as a guiding principle in helping to heal current cultural anomie and unrest; and to help determine the greatest good in any given situation, whether it be local or global.

Beauty is a common thread throughout all experience and backgrounds. The Way of Beauty is nonreligious and nonpolitical and intends no ethnic bias.

Practicing True Beauty will help evolve human consciousness.

Any individual can do it.

To help reclaim True Beauty, *start the sixteen practices today.*

Part Three

Reflecting on True Beauty

The Unity Paradox

All differences in this world are of degree, and not of kind, because oneness is the secret of everything."

— Swami Vivekananda

We are nudged and reminded time and again of our Oneness. While we are not the same we *are* individual nodes on the great Isness of Life. We forget this, and behave as if we are "other" and take actions that equate to the cultural version of shooting off our own feet. You know the ones I mean, and I am reminded of my mother admonishing my younger self, "Don't cut off your nose to spite your face!"

The Way of Beauty helps us avoid such silliness.

In our hearts we know that passing judgment on something is to become separate from it – to create that subject/object relationship which can nurture a divisive duality. In the observer-observed relationship we are creating separation, or more truly, the illusion of separation. Critical judgment, certain types of discernment, and evaluation lead us further into separation and the agreement to hold that illusion of separateness.

On the other hand, true compassion leads us to unity. We can celebrate our individual "unit-ness" while empathizing with the "other," seeing our reflection therein. We can own an awareness of our all being the same stuff, while embracing and enjoying the delightful individuation of that stuff.

In discussions where the concept of "unity awareness" or the phrase "we are all one" enters, often a skeptic will appear. Skepticism is expressed in any one of a variety of honest questions or concerns: "Duh! How can all be one?" "We don't *want* to all be the same do we?" "Do I look like anyone else?" "Isn't diversity a good thing?"

And of course we are not the same. Such misinterpretations of the Oneness concept can be traced to conceptual confusion of "oneness," "equality" and "sameness." The Eastern mystics were able to recognize individuality while at the same time holding an awareness of oneness of all *and* a sense of relative differences.

Fritjof Capra boiled this apparent dichotomy down to an elegant essence when he said:

"When the Eastern mystics tell us that they experience all things and events as manifestations of a basic oneness, this does not mean that they pronounce all things to be equal. They recognize the individuality of things, but at the same time they are aware that all differences and contrasts are relative within an all-embracing unity." (Capra, *The Tao of Physics.*)

We've been carried away by our individuality, individualism, individuated -- individu-whatevers -- into the illusion of separateness as reality. Yet there have been many analogies and descriptions of the many that make up the one – the cells of the body, the water molecules of the ocean, the individuals of a species.

In our culture at its current collective awareness level, it is easy for us humans to sense our individuality, our uniqueness that makes us feel separate and unique.

A potent visual of this idea is the ocean.

The wave appears separate, individuated from the rest of the ocean for a bit as it rises, crests, roils forth. It catches the light, sparkles, foams. It bends, it roars, it curves. A wave may gently lift aloft or crush with its great weight. It has great force. Each has its own form and character. The wave is its own event, isn't it?

Yet if one were to scoop out a cupful of that ocean, does that cup now contain the ocean? Has the ocean become damaged once the cupful is removed? It is in this sense that the one is wholly part of the whole, wholly. We rise and appear to stand apart for a period of time, then ebb and recede back into the whole. In harmony the entire time, though we may not fully perceive it, and at times it certainly may not feel it.

We are a beautiful ocean. We can change our tides.

As a wave is of the ocean – rising up, standing out, inexorably attracted toward air and the land, flowing swiftly towards it, finding it and then retreating back into the watery whole. Ebb and flow; rise and fall; reach and withdraw – these are the tides of the Universe.

Beauty Is the Raison D'Être of the Universe

I AM NOT alone in my suspicion that beauty is the *raison d'être* of our universe; Pseudo-Dionysius stated:

> For beauty is the cause of harmony, of sympathy, of community. Beauty unites all things and is the source of all things. It is the great creating cause which bestirs the world and holds all things in existence by the longing inside them to have beauty. And there it is ahead of all as...the Beloved...toward which all things move, since it is the longing for beauty which actually brings them into being. (Pseudo-Dionysius, *The Divine Names*, quoted by John O'Donohue in *Beauty, The Invisible Embrace.*)

I find so much evidence in the literature of quantum physics, other sciences, philosophy, folk wisdoms, and mythologies that points to the essential nature of True Beauty's role in our universe.

For instance, from the science and math camp—via a theologian—comes this little tidbit: "'Symmetry' is one of the most frequently recurring words in contemporary scientific literature." I add that *elegance* and *beautiful* would pop up repeatedly on the screen if anyone took the time to do a computerized word scan of current scientific and mathematical lectures and texts. Indeed, one of Brian Greene's most popular books is titled *The Elegant Universe.* And the Mandelbrot Set, or any fractals, when turned into computerized visuals, do not reveal jarring, disharmonious patterns, but beautiful ones.

I also find much anecdotal evidence simply by observing the world and its peoples: Beauty is the essence and manifests everywhere. It is the mother, daughter, and sacred spirit, to mess a bit with Christianity's trinity.

Only the *heart* can *intuit* the unmanifest level, the field of infinite possibilities. Our current science may not prove my hypothesis that the vibration that we call beauty is the source of the universe. Many religions, or faith, believe in love. My faith tells me that love is an outcome and a reaction to True Beauty.

And so to leap to a new definition of the *verb*:

> *Beauty is a dynamic process of becoming in the continuum of the universe, expressed in harmonic cyclical waves, rising into being, falling away—disintegrating into entropy, chaos, and discord—resolving again into orderly harmonies, emerging again, the universe unfurling, expanding, creating itself.*

This is how I understand the *action* of True Beauty. This is why it is a universally recognized entity among species, especially in the consciousness of man, and why it is *the* motivator. It is the essence of not only survival (maintenance) but birth (creation and expansion) and clearance (death)—perhaps as those memetics might like to have it, the main meme.

The Meta-Importance of True Beauty

The Zero Point Field might operate as a kind of "collective consciousness" [and]... it follows that humans can affect the world around them outside of space and time.

—Lynne McTaggart

Because of the "unseen" but powerful effects of intention, of fields—electromagnetic and other—and of the vibrations of human consciousness itself, awareness and practice of True Beauty makes a definitive difference. Through an *active practice of beauty,* we can evolve and expand our consciousness; gain greater ability to care for our home/planet; and be a productive, elegant, and facilitative element in the universe as it proceeds in its continual expansion and birthing of itself.

Attraction and relationship occur on nonmaterial planes. Relationships, those ubiquitous "horizons of belonging," are the glue of the universe; in harmony and discord, it is the creation, rearrangement, and maintenance of our Isness.

True, deep beauty is reflected in the life-force that is present all around us—it is a joyous, sometimes riotous party given by the entire universe. We are always invited, though too often we don't attend.

Look up, look around! Look out your window—there's a gorgeous party going on!

People…beauty is life when life unveils her holy face.
But you are life and you are the veil.
Beauty is eternity gazing at itself in a mirror.
But you are eternity and you are the mirror.

—Kahlil Gibran

Conclusion: Choices and the Hope for "A New Kind of Rationality"

Beauty is the practice that can heal humankind's present situation and return our world and our role within it to a positive and generative one.

EVERY SOCIETY HAS its methods to control its population. But is it possible that the fear and intimidation strategy is *backfiring*? Happily, I think so.

What will take its place?

History, in reviewing societal patterns and governmental orders, says the pendulum will swing back into conservatism, religious fundamentalism, perhaps even bondage, before the long cycles come around again to humanitarianism and democracy. We certainly are seeing signs of conservatism and religious fundamentalism in our culture and around the globe.

Yet what if we were brave enough, prescient enough, to opt out of these cyclical patterns? Is it even possible?

What if we were brave enough to believe in, trust, and have *faith* in, emulating the glorious authentic beauty around us, in the context in which it exists, embracing the entirety of *its* cycles—the birth, blossoming, ripening, and withering? Repeat. Repeat.

Repeat.

We are. We can. We *are* brave enough to burst into being out of the dark. To be unafraid of said dark or of death, without horrific statements of gloom and doom but instead in celebration of all the cycles, honoring them—much as has been seen in many tribal cultures around the globe.

What if we tried replacing fear and intimidation with inspiration and awe? With appreciation and awareness? With integrity and responsibility?

Engaging with beauty helps to reverse the current toxic flow. It flies in the face of the mass media's "hyperbole of the horrific" and reclaims sanity and common sense. It is in sync with chaos, oxymoron notwithstanding.

It is patently clear that our comfy ol' "age of reason" approach is no longer, er…reasonable. It has created, and is no longer working with, the myriad conundrums we are facing in our modern world.

We are evolving as conscious entities. We can choose deep compassion and embrace beauty as the force and source and stuff of oneness. The one and the zero, the point, and the monad exist only in relation and reflection of one another. That relationship, that relativity is expressed in a field of resonance that in synergy is True Beauty. In discord, it is the creative chaos that mixes up and unfurls—eventually births—new beauty.

Embrace beauty as that force, field, and continuum of resonance darkly spinning, unfurling, and vibrating. Be party to it!

I humbly suggest that the reclamation of True Beauty and its concrete integration into our value sets and daily operational lives is an extremely viable alternative, one that will create balance in and between our techie world and our famished souls. It's an alternative that puts the power for positive change into *our* hands.

To imagine beauty is to create beauty.

This Shaman's View

We are dreaming the world into being. This dreaming is not only a sleep and nighttime activity. We are all blessed with imagination, and that imagination fuels and informs our dreams, whether they be daydreams, sleep dreams, or swift "flights of fancy," as we go through the activities of our days.

Imagination fills in the details.

Imagination builds our reality.

Let us imagine beauty. Let us dream of beauty. Let us create beauty all around.

Imagination is more important than knowledge.
For knowledge is limited to all we
now know and understand,
while imagination embraces the entire world, and
all there ever will be to know and understand.

—Albert Einstein

With beauty may I walk.
With beauty before me may I walk.
With beauty behind me may I walk.
With beauty above me may I walk.
With beauty all around me may I walk.
In old age wandering on a trail of beauty,
lively, may I walk.
In old age wandering on a trail of beauty,
living again, may I walk.
It is finished in beauty.
It is finished in beauty.
—Prayer, Night Way (Navajo)

The End?

To paraphrase Paul Valery:
No artist ever finishes a piece of work, (s)he merely abandons it.

Acknowledgments

BEAUTY AS ACTION: *How Practicing True Beauty Can Change Our World* has been in the works for a decade. The encouragement and support of many strong and wise women has been in large part what has helped to finally birth this book. Like patient and knowledgeable midwives, these friends have been there at the right moment in the process, articulating and sharing exactly what was needed to facilitate the next stage in what was a rather long gestation period, and, finally, what has felt like a birthing event to me—the publication of this book. I must mention a few of these women.

It is with deep gratitude that I thank Theresa Dintino for her probing questions and spiritual support and Markey Read for her continual belief in me. To both Polly Smith and Rebecca Brookes, I am grateful for their steadfast friendship and the layered perspectives only very long friendships can bring. The many discussions I've had with each of these women have stirred my cauldron of creativity using the sturdy spoon of perseverance!

Thanks to Jessica Swift, dedicated editor. And many thanks to Heather Powers, artist and organizer extraordinaire, who has been so very helpful in the latest chapter of my life. I could not have done this last trimester without her encouragement and help. Heck, I might not have been able to *find* my manuscript!

And then there are two women who helped me see, really *see,* but in very different ways. First is the late Judith Fortune Koplewitz, a very loving and wise woman who helped me to see not only the layers of relationship but also to come to deeply understand my responsibility in them. The second is my sister, Victoria Z. Woodrow. A lifelong and talented artist, she taught her little sister to see with an artist's eyes. It was she who first showed me those pinks in the "green" grass.

With such smart, inquiring, and humorous women in our world, our earth will be all right. Thank you all—I couldn't have made it through the birthing process without you and your bright minds and quick wits. We laughed our way to press!

L. Lindahl
Charleston, South Carolina
August 2017

A book is a dream that you hold in your hand.
—Neil Gaiman

Notes

A Manifesto for True Beauty

ALFRED NORTH WHITEHEAD (1861–1947) was a British mathematician and philosopher. He is the father of the philosophical school known as "*process philosophy,*"[18] which has influenced a wide variety of disciplines (such as physics, theology, education, and ecology) and a broad range of thinkers and doers (Bertrand Russell, David Bohm, William Temple). A bit dense to read, but a truly original thinker. Worth the effort.

James Hillman (1926–2011) may be called an American psychologist, but he was so much more—a great thinker who delved beyond Jungian thought and into the imaginal. He noted that after a hundred years of psychoanalysis, we were only getting worse. To sample some of his thought, check out *Blue Fire* (with Thomas Moore) or *The Soul's Code: On Character and Calling*; online find his excellent article, "Virtues of Caution," *Resurgence Magazine*, Issue 213, July/Aug 2002.

Elaine Scarry (born 1946). I am forever grateful to Prof. Scarry. I discovered her book, *On Beauty and Being Just*, early in my investigation of beauty. It was inspiring and provocative. She is professor of aesthetics and general theory of value at Harvard University.

Sociopolitical Need for Beauty

John O'Donohue (1956–2008). My first guide on this journey! In his excellent book, *Beauty, the Invisible Embrace,* O'Donohue has done an eloquent job making the case tying the decline of beauty to the degradation of our culture. I cannot say enough about this great poet and philosopher. His insistence upon the importance of beauty, his gnowingness of the divine all around, inspired and transformed me as well as countless others. He is one of my heroes.

To Gnow

Thomas Berry, CP, PhD (1914–2009). He was a priest and "Earth scholar," or *geologian* as he preferred to be called. A leading voice in ecospirituality and the "New Story," he proposed that a deep understanding of the history and functioning of the universe is necessary for our own successful *spiritual* evolution.

Thomas Berry's book, *The Dream of the Earth,* was a groundbreaking (no pun intended) work for the environmental movement. A chapter in it, "A New Story," inspired many to take action. Brian Swimme, author, educator, and mathematical cosmologist, worked closely with Berry toward the end of his life.

Both/And Practice

The "giant ball" illustration was something I learned from a consultant while in business, although I don't remember who/when. Although I may have embellished or changed it over the years, as I have repeated it often, it is not my original thought.

Practice Compassion

More information regarding brain-imaging studies and the ability to feel compassion may be found at the University of Wisconsin–Madison's Waisman Center for Brain Imaging (Richard Davidson, director), or the Fetzer Foundation, fetzer.org. There are other sources as well.

Think with Heart

Info and studies of the intriguing powers and dynamics of our hearts now abound. (They did not when this book was first being formed). One go-to place is the HeartMath Institute. When I first found it online, it had a bunch of research data for free, just available to review and mine. It was a fabulous eye and mind opener. Now it is much more sophisticated and has techie tools, training programs, and so on. It is organized and branded and has a lot of info for sale. Much of the information I use in this book is from its long-ago days. I don't know if the links I cite are even still available. The data, however, can still be checked with HeartMath.

Be Wary of the Truth

The aestheticism movement in Europe and America in the late 1800s caused quite a stir. One on-line definition (ArtLex.com, 2007) has it as "the belief that the pursuit of beauty is the most important goal, and that it is the artist's duty to orchestrate... elements from nature into a composition that...exists for its own sake, without regard to moral or didactic issues."

Practice Authenticity

I met Dr. David Simon at the Chopra Center in Southern California, where he was cofounder with Dr. Chopra. Fascinating to me, he was trained as a neurologist; during his tenure at the Chopra Center, he specialized in Ayurvedic and mind-body medicine. He was a very articulate and excellent teacher.

Lucius Seneca, or "Seneca the Younger," was a first-century CE Roman philosopher, politician, and humorist.

Self-Acceptance

For families and people with epilepsy, the advocacy organization to go to is the Epilepsy Foundation, www.epilepsy.com, an extensive and informative site. I am proud to say I was on its Board of Directors for nine years.

Deborah Grassman, nurse and spokesperson for Opus Peace (opuspeace.org), works primarily with veterans for the healing necessary beyond the merely physical. The organization works with those suffering from PTSD as well the less acknowledged yet deeply damaging *soul injury.*

Harmonic Relationships

David Bohm (1917–1992) was a fascinating character! If, like me, you didn't have the good fortune to learn about him in school, consider learning about him now. A theoretical physicist, his list of contributions is almost unbelievable. McCarthyism threw this American-born genius out of the United States during that dark period of our nation's history. Even colleague Albert Einstein's support did not help him. Check him out.

Nonlocal and *nonlocality* are terms for a concept I first bumped into when I started practicing meditation and delving into the shamanic realms. I imagine many people these days now learn about it in their quantum physics or web development classes. This concept of nonlocality and its sibling, entanglement, challenges how we have understood our cosmos and "reality" in the past: the speed of light is *not* the fastest in the universe; there are what Einstein called "spooky actions at a distance" when items in far distant parts of the universe can know instantaneously about one another. The entrance of the dynamic of the *nonlocal* into modern science has afforded greater insight to me, and perhaps others, into actions and possibilities of spiritual realms.

Anomie is a great word that encapsulates a complex concept of a society's alienation. The dictionary definition says, "The social instability resulting from a breakdown of standards and values; *also*: personal unrest, alienation, and uncertainty that comes from a lack of purpose or ideals."

K.I.S.S. Practice

Myth of Indra's Net:

Indra's net is an excellent example of a complex concept made almost instantly understandable through the elegant simplicity of a graphic illustration.

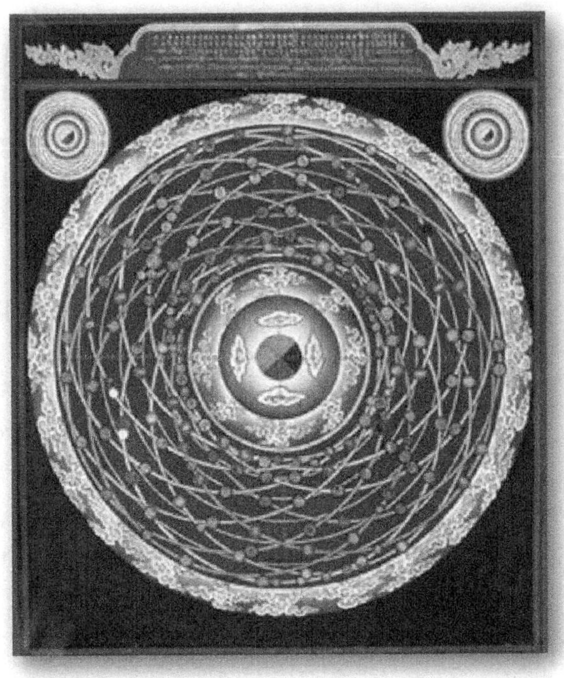

Far away in the heavenly abode of the great god Indra, there is a wonderful net which has been hung by some cunning artificer in such a manner that it stretches out indefinitely in all directions. In accordance with the extravagant tastes of deities, the artificer has hung a single glittering jewel at the net's every node, and since the net itself is infinite in dimension, the jewels are infinite in number. There hang the jewels, glittering like stars of the first magnitude, a wonderful sight to behold. If we now arbitrarily select one of these jewels for inspection and look closely at it, we will discover that in its polished surface there are reflected all the other jewels in the net, infinite in number. Not only that, but each of the jewels reflected in this one jewel is also reflecting all the other jewels, so that the process of reflection is infinite.

—Avatamsaka Sutra

One of the best word explanations of Indra's Net comes from Richard Lubbock, in his fun *Alfred North Whitehead, Philosopher for the Muddleheaded,* where he paraphrased Whitehead:

> "The doctrine of The Jewel Net of Indra...teaches that the cosmos is like an infinite network of glittering jewels, all different. In each one we can see the images of all the others reflected. Each image contains an image of all the other jewels; and also the image of the images of the images and so ad infinitum. The myriad reflections within each jewel are the essence of the jewel itself, without which it does not exist...every part of the cosmos reflects, and brings into existence, every other part. Nothing can exist unless it enfolds within its essence the nature of everything else."

I love this visualization of concept of oneness. I love how ancient it is. It is an elegant, simple illustration of a very complex idea: not only of the many of the one but also of a holographic universe.

Practice Creation

Gary J. Witherspoon (born 1943), is a non-Navajo scholar who is fluent in the Navajo language. He wrote of the Navajo culture in *Language and Art in the Navajo Universe.* It was in this extensive and sensitive work that I first learned how a beauty-centric culture had indeed manifested and thrived. It gave me hope and fed my imagination with what another might look like in the here and the now.

Trade and Commerce
Title IX: "No person in the United States shall, on the basis of sex, be excluded from participation in, be denied the benefits of, or be subjected to discrimination under any education program or activity receiving federal financial assistance." Essentially, Title IX prohibits sex discrimination in educational institutions that receive federal funding (the vast majority of schools).

The doctrine of anima mundi is originally Greek from Plato: World Soul.

Supporting Practices
The Universal Declaration of Human Rights was created in post–World War II in 1948 and championed by Eleanor Roosevelt. Additional covenants were attached, and in 1976, it became international law as the International Covenant on Economic, Social, and Cultural Rights. The full text is available on the United Nations website at www.un.org/en/universal-declaration-human-rights.

As they bear repeating these days, here are the original thirty articles:

> Article 1. All human beings are born free and equal in dignity and rights. They are endowed with reason and conscience and should act toward one another in a spirit of brotherhood.
>
> Article 2. Everyone is entitled to all the rights and freedoms set forth in this Declaration, without distinction of any kind, such as race, colour, sex, language, religion, political or other opinion, national or social origin, property,

birth or other status. Furthermore, no distinction shall be made on the basis of the political, jurisdictional or international status of the country or territory to which a person belongs, whether it be independent, trust, non-self-governing or under any other limitation of sovereignty.

Article 3. Everyone has the right to life, liberty and security of person.

Article 4. No one shall be held in slavery or servitude; slavery and the slave trade shall be prohibited in all their forms.

Article 5. No one shall be subjected to torture or to cruel, inhuman or degrading treatment or punishment

Article 6. Everyone has the right to recognition everywhere as a person before the law.

Article 7. All are equal before the law and are entitled without any discrimination to equal protection of the law. All are entitled to equal protection against any discrimination in violation of this Declaration and against any incitement to such discrimination.

Article 8. Everyone has the right to an effective remedy by the competent national tribunals for acts violating the fundamental rights granted him by the constitution or by law.

Article 9. No one shall be subjected to arbitrary arrest, detention or exile.

Article 10. Everyone is entitled in full equality to a fair and public hearing by an independent and impartial tribunal, in the determination of his rights and obligations and of any criminal charge against him.

Article 11. 1. Everyone charged with a penal offence has the right to be presumed innocent until proved guilty according to law in a public trial at which he has had all the guarantees necessary for his defense. 2. No one shall be held guilty of any penal offence on account of any act or omission which did not constitute a penal offence, under national or international law, at the time when it was committed. Nor shall a heavier penalty be imposed than the one that was applicable at the time the penal offence was committed.

Article 12. No one shall be subjected to arbitrary interference with his privacy, family, home or correspondence, nor to attacks upon his honour and reputation. Everyone has the right to the protection of the law against such interference or attacks.

Article 13. 1. Everyone has the right to freedom of movement and residence within the borders of each state. 2. Everyone has the right to leave any country, including his own, and to return to his country.

Article 14. 1. Everyone has the right to seek and to enjoy in other countries asylum from persecution. 2. This right may not be invoked in the case of prosecutions genuinely arising from nonpolitical crimes or from acts contrary to the purposes and principles of the United Nations.

Article 15. 1. Everyone has the right to a nationality. 2. No one shall be arbitrarily deprived of his nationality nor denied the right to change his nationality.

Article 16. 1. Men and women of full age, without any limitation due to race, nationality or religion, have the right to marry and to found a family. They are entitled to equal rights as to marriage, during marriage and at its dissolution. 2. Marriage shall be entered into only with the free and full consent of the intending spouses. 3. The family is the natural and fundamental group unit of society and is entitled to protection by society and the State.

Article 17. 1. Everyone has the right to own property alone as well as in association with others. 2. No one shall be arbitrarily deprived of his property.

Article 18. Everyone has the right to freedom of thought, conscience and religion; this right includes freedom to change his religion or belief, and freedom, either alone or in community with others and in public or private, to manifest his religion or belief in teaching, practice, worship and observance.

Article 19. Everyone has the right to freedom of opinion and expression; this right includes freedom to hold opinions without interference and to seek, receive and impart information and ideas through any media and regardless of frontiers.

Article 20. 1. Everyone has the right to freedom of peaceful assembly and association. 2. No one may be compelled to belong to an association.

Article 21. 1. Everyone has the right to take part in the government of his country, directly or through freely chosen representatives. 2. Everyone has the right of equal access to public service in his country. 3. The will of the people shall be the basis of the authority of government; this will shall be expressed in periodic and genuine elections which shall be by universal and equal suffrage and shall be held by secret vote or by equivalent free voting procedures.

Article 22. Everyone, as a member of society, has the right to social security and is entitled to realization, through national effort and international co-operation and in accordance with the organization and resources of each State, of the economic, social and cultural rights indispensable for his dignity and the free development of his personality.

Article 23. 1. Everyone has the right to work, to free choice of employment, to just and favourable conditions of work and to protection against unemployment. 2. Everyone, without any discrimination, has the right to equal pay for equal work. 3. Everyone who works has the right to just and favourable remuneration ensuring for himself and his family an existence worthy of human dignity, and supplemented, if necessary, by other means of social protection. 4. Everyone has the right to form and to join trade unions for the protection of his interests.

Article 24. Everyone has the right to rest and leisure, including reasonable limitation of working hours and periodic holidays with pay.

Article 25. 1. Everyone has the right to a standard of living adequate for the health and well-being of himself and of his family, including food, clothing, housing and medical care and necessary social services, and the right to security in the event of unemployment, sickness, disability, widowhood, old age or other lack of livelihood in circumstances beyond his control. 2. Motherhood and childhood are entitled to special care and assistance. All children, whether born in or out of wedlock, shall enjoy the same social protection.

Article 26. 1. Everyone has the right to education. Education shall be free, at least in the elementary and fundamental stages. Elementary education shall be compulsory. Technical and professional education shall be made generally available and higher education shall be equally accessible to all on the basis of merit. 2. Education shall be directed to the full development of the human personality and to the strengthening of respect for human rights and fundamental freedoms. It shall promote understanding, tolerance and friendship among all nations, racial or religious groups, and shall further the activities of the United Nations for the maintenance of peace. 3. Parents have a prior right to choose the kind of education that shall be given to their children.

Article 27. 1. Everyone has the right freely to participate in the cultural life of the community, to enjoy the arts and to share in scientific advancement and its benefits. 2. Everyone has the right to the protection of the moral and material interests resulting from any scientific, literary or artistic production of which he is the author.

Article 28. Everyone is entitled to a social and international order in which the rights and freedoms set forth in this Declaration can be fully realized.

Article 29. 1. Everyone has duties to the community in which alone the free and full development of his personality is possible. 2. In the exercise of his rights and freedoms, everyone shall be subject only to such limitations as are determined by law solely for the purpose of securing due recognition and respect for the rights and freedoms of others and of meeting the just requirements of morality, public order and the general welfare in a democratic society. 3. These rights and freedoms may in no case be exercised contrary to the purposes and principles of the United Nations.

Article 30. Nothing in this Declaration may be interpreted as implying for any State, group or person any right to engage in any activity or to perform any act aimed at the destruction of any of the rights and freedoms set forth herein.

Selected Bibliography

Ballou, Mary, and Nancy W. Gabalac. *A Feminist Theory On Mental Health.* Springfield, IL: Charles C. Thomas, 1985.

Beckley, Bill, ed. *Uncontrollable Beauty: Toward a New Aesthetics.* New York: Allworth Press, 1998.

Berry, Thomas. *The Dream of the Earth.* San Francisco: Sierra Club Books, 1990.

Briggs, John, and David Peat. *Seven Life Lessons of Chaos: Spiritual Wisdom from the Science of Change.* New York: HarperPerennial, 2000.

Cameron, Julia. *The Artist's Way: A Spiritual Path to Higher Creativity.* New York: G. P. Putnam's Sons, 1992.

———. *Some People Say That…God Is No Laughing Matter.* New York: Tarcher/Putnam, 2001.

———. *Vein of Gold: A Journey to Your Creative Heart.* New York: Jeremy P. Tarcher/Putnam, 1996.

———. *Walking in this World.* New York: Jeremy P. Tarcher/Putnam, 2002.

Campbell, Joseph. *The Inner Reaches of Outer Space: Metaphor as Myth and as Religion.* New York: Alfred Van Der Marck Edition, 1985.

Cannato, Judy. *Field of Compassion.* Notre Dame, IN: Sorin Books, 2010.

Chopra, Deepak. *The Book of Secrets.* New York: Harmony Books, 2004.

———. *The Seven Spiritual Laws of Success.* San Rafael, CA: Amber-Allen Publishing, 1993.

———. *The Way of the Wizard.* New York: Harmony Books, 1995.

Conlon, James. *The Sacred Impulse.* New York: The Crossroad Publishing, 2000.

Easwaran, Eknath, trans. *The Upanishads.* Tomales, CA: Nilgiri Press, 2007.

Eliade, Mircea. *Essential Sacred Writings from around the World.* New York: HarperCollins, 1967.

Estes, Clarissa Pinkola. *Women Who Run with the Wolves: Myths and Stories of the Wild Woman Archetype.* New York: Ballantine Books, 1992.

Foster, Rick, and Greg Hicks. *How We Choose to Be Happy: The 9 Choices of Extremely Happy People—Their Secrets, Their Stories.* New York: Berkeley Publishing Group, 2004.

Fox, Matthew. *Creativity.* New York: Jeremy P. Tarcher/Penguin, 2004.

Ghiselin, Brewster, ed. *The Creative Process: A Symposium.* New York: Signet, The New American Library, 1952.

Gold, Taro. *Living Wabi Sabi: The True Beauty of Your Life.* Kansas City, MO: Andrews McMeel Publishing, 2004.

Greene, Brian. *The Elegant Universe.* Vintage Books, 2000.

Harner, Michael. *The Way of the Shaman.*

Harvey, Andrew. *The Return of the Mother.* Berkeley, CA: Frog, Ltd., 1995.

Hawken, Paul. *Blessed Unrest.* New York: Penguin Group, 2007.

Jarrett, James L. *The Quest for Beauty.* Englewood Cliffs, NJ: Prentice-Hall, 1957.

Kant, I. *The Critique of Judgment.* Translated by J. C. Meredith. Oxford: Oxford University Press, 1964.

Keen, Sam. *The Passionate Life.* San Francisco: Harper, 1983.

Kierkegaard, Soren. *Works of Love.* Translated by Howard and Edna Hong. New York: Harper & Row, 1962.

Koren, Leonard. *Wabi-Sabi for Artists, Designers, Poets, and Philosophers.* Berkeley, CA: Stone Bridge Press, 1994.

Korten, David C. *The Great Turning: From Empire to Earth Community.* San Francisco, CA: Berret-Koehler Publishers, 2005.

Maeda, John. *The Laws of Simplicity.* Cambridge, MA: MIT Press, 2006.

Marx Hubbard, Barbara. *Emergence.* San Francisco: Hampton Roads Publishing Company, 2012.

May, Rollo. *The Courage to Create.* New York: Bantam Books, 1975.

———. *Love and Will.* New York: Dell Publishing, 1969.

———. *My Quest For Beauty.* Dallas, TX: Saybrook, 1985.

McTaggart, Lynne. *The Field: The Quest for the Secret Force of the Universe.* New York: HarperCollins, 2002.

Moore, Thomas. *Care of the Soul.* New York: HarperPerennial, 1992.

———. *The Re-enchantment of Everyday Life.* New York: HarperPerennial, 1997.

Nepo, Mark. *The Exquisite Risk: Daring to Live an Authentic Life.* New York: Three Rivers Press, 2005.

O'Donohue, John. *Beauty, the Invisible Embrace.* New York: HarperCollins, 2005.

O'Murchu, Diarmud. *Quantum Theology: Spiritual Implications of the New Physics.* New York: The Crossroad Publishing Company, 2004.

O'Shaughnessy, Ann, ed. *The Heron Dance: Book of Love and Gratitude.* North Ferrisburg, VT: Heron Dance Press, 2005.

Safina, Carl. *Beyond Words.* Picador/Henry Holt and Co., 2015.

Sartwell, Crispin. *Six Names of Beauty.* New York: Routledge, 2004.

Scarry, Elaine, *On Beauty and Being Just.* Princeton, NJ: Princeton University Press, 1999.

Serevan-Schreiber, Jean-Louis. *The Art of Time.* Addison-Wesley Publishing.

Simon, David. *The Ten Commitments: Translating Good Intentions into Great Choices.* Deerfield Beach, FL: Health Communications, 2006.

Talbot, Michael. *The Holographic Universe.* New York: Harper Perennial, 1992.

Vaughan, Frances. *Shadows of the Sacred: Seeing through Spiritual Illusions.* Lincoln, NE: iUniverse, 2005.

Walker, Alice. *We Are the Ones We Have Been Waiting For.* New York: The New Press, 2006.

Weitz, Morris. *Problems in Aesthetics.* New York: The Macmillan Company, 1959.

Whitehead, Alfred North. *Adventures of Ideas.* Simon & Schuster, 1933, 1967.

Witherspoon, Gary. *Language and Art in the Navajo Universe.* University of Michigan Press, 1977.

Zukav, Gary. *The Seat of the Soul.* New York: Simon & Schuster, 1989.

Internet References

"Aesthetic Movement." www.ArtLex.com.

Charter for Compassion. www.charterforcompassion.org.

Declaration for Human Rights. http://www.un.org/en/universal-declaration-human-rights/index.html.

Gracyk, Ted. "Hume's Aesthetics." The Stanford Encyclopedia of Philosophy, Edward N. Zalta, ed. (Winter 2006 edition).

"Head-Heart Interactions." www.heartmath.org/research/science-of-the-heart/soh_20.html.

Hillman, James. "The Virtues of Caution: A Call to Awaken Our Aesthetic Responses." *Resurgence Magazine,* Issue 213.

Institute of HeartMath. www.heartmath.org/research/research-intuition/overview.html.

Pitts, Soni. "H is for Hozho," in "ABCs of a Great Life." EzineArticles.com.

Some Further Reading

Abram, David. *The Spell of the Sensuous.* New York: Vintage Books, 1997

Arnheim, R. *Art and Visual Perception.* Berkeley: University of California Press, 1954.

Beardsley, M. C. *Aesthetics.* New York: Harcourt Brace, 1958.

Crawford, D. W. *Kant's Aesthetic Theory.* Madison: University of Wisconsin Press, 1974.

Dickie, G. *The Century of Taste.* Oxford: Oxford University Press, 1996.

Dintino, Theresa. *Teachings from the Trees,* 2016.

Graham, G. *Philosophy of the Arts: An Introduction to Aesthetics.* London: Routledge, 1997.

Hanfling, O., ed. *Philosophical Aesthetics.* Oxford: Blackwell, 1992.

Hjort, M., and S. Laver, eds. *Emotion and the Arts.* Oxford University Press, 1997.

Huddle, Norie. *Butterfly.* Huddle Publishing, 1990. (This is the original story of transformation that has spread widely throughout social media.)

Mothersill, M. *Beauty Restored.* Oxford: Clarendon, 1984.

Nepo, Mark. *The Book of Awakening.* San Francisco: Conari Press, 2011.

Ruiz, Miguel. *The Four Agreements.* San Rafael, CA: Amber-Allen Publishing, 1997.

Taylor, R. *Beyond Art.* Brighton: Harvester, 1981.

Williams, Florence. *The Nature Fix.* New York: W. W. Norton, 2017.

Made in the USA
Middletown, DE
24 January 2020